The Colors of Voices

The Colors of Voices

Dave Love

DEDICATION

I dedicate this writing to my mother and my friend, Jackie McCoy, and to the Oldies Show, and my other close friends.

TABLE OF CONTENTS

INTRODUCTION

In 1979, in a fork lift accident on my grandfather's farm, I lost my senses of sight, smell, and taste, and suffered a brain injury as well. Although I didn't realize it at the time, I also gained something, something most people regard as remarkable if they believe me. It is something no one can see, smell, taste, or touch, but we all hear it. It is something I am so familiar with that it has become second nature to me.

I am talking about the colors of voices, the outline of a voice and how they are made up. There is no right or wrong answer to a voice color, and there is nothing good or bad about the color that the voice makes up. This is called synesthesia, colors and shapes, two senses somehow blending into one in the brain.

The idea of synesthesia was published for the first time as long ago as 1880 in an article by Francis Galton, a cousin of Charles Darwin. For a long time, researchers concluded that this was a fictitious phenomenon. However, current research shows that it is genuine. Researchers today believe that anywhere from one in 200 up to one in 100,000 has this unique ability. For relying on my memories of colors, this too has a name, and it is called the Charles Bonnet syndrome. From research shows, the part of the brain, that controls, the vision, does not work anymore for someone like me, that cannot see. This creates phantom images of things in the mind in colors of things you remember, before the loss of sight. These two attributes, hearing and memory, work together to provide the colors I hear in voices.

The first time I meet a person and hear his or her regular voice, I picture things in my mind concerning the voice, which I will go into later; but for now, I will say that all voices are based on the color white. Some show their whiteness more than others; it depends on the density of each voice. There are many white sounds, but the human voice is the original.

A doorbell's sound is red, always the same color for every doorbell that rings, even though its sound travels to the ear in two intervals: ding-dong. The second interval is darker than the first interval on the doorbell. If the sound were blue, the boundaries would be different. When I do hear a doorbell, I always think of Avon, or the song from Wizard of Oz, "Ding-Dong the Witch Is Dead". A phone at the college I attended rang with a red sound. I answered that phone for the Development Department during lunch. The phone's ring was red, but wet, as if it came from under the water, like bubbles coming from underneath the water. How I hear this, I do not know. Many people think of red as a color signifying danger, while green seems safer. Maybe we have come to these conclusions because of traffic lights. The sound of a phone ringing is only one sound, but the chimes that I have in my home make all sorts of sounds at once and they are all silver, no matter how the wind blows.

It is like tools being moved in a tool box, the bigger the box, the deeper silver sound you get. I remember a lot of tools are silver in color. If your chimes have different lengths and sizes, the more musical silver sound you get. Whatever strikes or rings has its own sound, and the sound has its own color. For example, if the chimes are made out of glass, this sounds blue. This sound by itself sounds like a music box. For me, all music boxes have the color sound blue, no matter what notes they play. Of course this is meant to relax you while you are listening. The frequency's high notes of the music box give it the feel of the color blue. If the chimes are made out of wood, I picture percussion instruments like the wood block or *castanets* that make up the color brown, like some bark on the trees. A grandfather clock's chimes sound gold, a regular size. The smaller the clock, the lighter the sound. The smaller sound has a white glow, making it gold-white. The big ones have a darker sound, gold-black. Of course the black glow is the size of the darker ring, even with the other notes that are audible. But on the piano each note has its own color. On the grandfather clock chimes make the sound, while a hammer with strings makes the piano's noise. When I picture the grandfather clock in my head, I can see the pendulum gold, and the hands on the clock itself are gold, with a brown casing around it. This is the kind of grandfather clock I remember seeing back in the 1970's.

Sound travels differently for each color. It differs with the shape, width, length, narrowness, or wideness of the sound, but the echo in a sound has no effect on it. The voice, however, does.

I can tell when people I know are feeling under the weather because their voices are a little bit lower than usual and have a different quality to them, quieter. When people are under stress, I hear it in their voices, although there is sometimes confusion because laughing and crying sound alike. However, I have learned that, if I listen very, very closely, laughter does not last as long as crying.

Chapter One:
DEFINING COLORS

     Within sound travels the light and energy of colors. Not the way sunlight travels, but the colors in the rainbow without light, the spectrum from sunlight, which includes red, orange, yellow, green, blue, indigo, and violet. This is a refracting white light with a prism dissolving into its component attributes. It was discovered by Sir Isaac Newton in his 1666 to 1672 experiments. Before, everyone thought color was a mixture of light and darkness and that prisms were colored light. The color theory scale that went from brilliant red appeared to be pure white light with the least amount of darkness added, and then to dull blue. This appeared to be the last step before black, which was the dead end, where light is extinguished by darkness. Now, thanks to Newton, we know that light alone is responsible for color.

     With light, there are different wave lengths: x-rays, ultraviolet, infrared, microwave, and radio waves. Then you have the different kinds of lamps, like the Tungsten lamp, and common ordinary light bulbs, also the fluorescent lamps, and the tube light bulbs, and arc lamps, the neon, mercury, or other gas filled lamps. You cannot perceive the light that I am using since is not apparent to the eye. Light is not the same to the ear.

     To understand, you must consider the wavelength interval and frequency interval of colors. The wavelength interval has to do with the distance traveled, like throwing a rock in to the pond. Wavelength intervals are measured in nanometers, abbreviated nm. Frequency means the number of occurrences of a repeated event per unit. The period is the duration of one cycle in a repeated event and is, therefore, the reciprocal of the frequency. It is measured in hertz, abbreviated Hz, or terahertz, THz. Now, here are the colors with the different wavelengths intervals, and the different frequency intervals:

- Red wavelength interval is 700-630 nm, and the frequency interval is 430-480 Hz.
- For the color orange, the wavelength interval 630-590 nm, and the frequency interval is 480-510 THz.
- Yellow has a wavelength interval of 590-560 nm, and the frequency interval is 510-540 THz.
- For green, the wavelength interval is 560-490 nm, and the frequency interval is 540-610 THz.
- Blue is 490-450 nm, and 610-670 THz.
- Violet is 450-400 nm, and 670-750 THz.

Sunlight is a form of energy. We feel how warm the sun is outside, especially in August. The color, wavelength, frequency and energy of light are composed of particles called photons. The visible light of electromagnetic radiation is the atom. Electrons moving in orbits that go around the nucleus of an atom are arranged in different energy levels within their electron clouds. By this, the electron can gather other energy from outside sources of electromagnetic radiation. This graduates to a higher energy level.

Higher energies are thought of as having shorter wavelengths and lower energies are thought of as having higher wavelengths. The energy of a photon is linked proportionally to its frequency and, inversely, is proportional to its wavelength. Very high frequency electromagnetic radiation, like gamma rays, X-rays, and ultraviolet light, is controlled by very short wavelengths and, therefore, a great deal of energy. Then you have lower frequency radiation, like the visible, infrared, microwave, and radio waves, all having greater wavelengths, but matching the lower frequencies and energy.

Electromagnetic radiation is built up by its wavelength or frequency and its intensity. The wavelength reaches the visible spectrum and then you can see the visible light. This is equal to 380 nm to 740 nm. A lot of the light sources get in at many different wavelengths, a source's spectrum giving its intensity at each wavelength. The given direction of the light to the eye determines the color sensation. Also, in that same direction, are many more possible spectral combinations than color sensations. If there is a low intensity on the color, orange-yellow will be brown. A low intensity on yellow-green will result in olive-green. An object's color depends on much more than its viewer's eye and brain; it is also due to the physics of the object itself and its environment.

The reflective properties of the surface of an object work hand in hand with the angles of illumination to determine the color of the object. The spectrum of the light depends on how much light an object reflects and contextual cues being relatively constant. This is called color constancy. There are two types: absorbed and opaque and they each determine the way the light makes the objects appear.

Research has shown, there has been estimated that there are about 10 million colors perceivable by a human being, but more than 16 million colors in existence. Take, for example, blue-yellows or red-greens. These colors are opposite of each other and make up the basis of color vision. Ewald Hering was the first to come up with color vision back in the 19th century.

Later on, a color chart was developed, on which all colors are derived from a measure of green, red, blue, and yellow with varied brightness. To shade a color, to make it darker, you add black; to add a tint to a color and make it lighter, you add white. Thus, the value of each color will be lighter or darker.

Chapter Two:
THE EYE

It is important to consider how light travels through the eye in order to determine the color of an object. "Perfect vision," or normal visual acuity, is determined to be 20:20, which basically means that one can clearly see at a distance of 20 feet what one should see at that distance. When wavelengths are visible light to a human eye, the range perceived is around 390nm to 750hm.

Focusing on the part of the eye that deals with light, the outer layer is called the cornea. This is a dome shaped structure at the front of the eye that allows light to enter the eye. Together with the lens, the cornea helps focus and direct light onto the retina, which I will discuss further below.

The iris is the middle layer of the eye, or the colored part of the eye. It controls the size of the pupil, the black area in the center of the iris. If you walk outside in bright sunlight, the iris reduces the pupil's size to restrict the amount of light entering the eye. If you enter a dark room, the iris opens up the pupil to allow more light in.

The lens is a clear, flexible structure that changes shape so that you can focus on objects at different distances. When you look at objects that are far away in the distance, the ciliary muscles in the eye relax, making the lens thinner. When you inspect an object up close, the lens becomes thicker and curved and the ciliary muscles shrink in size.

The vitreous humor is located behind the lens. It is a jelly-like substance that fills in the back of the eye, helping it to keep its shape and aiding in the transmission of light.

The choroid is a membrane found before the retina. It contains a lot of blood vessels that bring oxygen and nutrients to the retina. This highly pigmented part of the eye helps to take in the light and prevent it from scattering.

Now we get to the inner layer of the eye, the retina. It outlines the back of the eye and is highly light-sensitive with millions of cells called photoreceptors. Each photoreceptor connects to a nerve fiber and all the nerve fibers form the optic nerve. There are two photoreceptors: the rods and cones. The rods are more sensitive than the cones, but they are not sensitive to color. The cones determine color receptivity. Color blindness results when a person is lacking some of the cones that are normally present in the eye. Even missing just one cone will diminish color receptivity. Red and green are the most common colors involved in color blindness.

One part of the photoreceptors is the macula, a small area of the retina that has a high concentration of cone cells. It gives you sharp central vision. Once an image is picked up by the photoreceptors, the information is changed to nerve impulses by the optic nerve and sent to the brain.

There are three types of color receptor cells or cones in the retina. First are the short-wavelength cones that make the color violet visible, with wavelengths around 420nm. Sometimes they are misleadingly called the blue cones. The second and third are closely related. The long-wavelength cones make the color red visible and are very sensitive to light. Interestingly enough, this visible light is perceived as yellowish-green wavelengths around 564nm. Then comes the middle-wavelength cones, the wavelengths around 534nm also sometimes misleadingly called the green cones because in the visible light they are perceived as green. These three types of cones send out three signals, making three locations and three color components in the eye, sometimes called tristimulus values. If the middle-wavelength cones are activated in the present moment, the other cones take part in it too, but only to a certain degree.

After the color goes through the eye, the information of the color is communicated to the brain by three contending processes. First is the red-green channel. Second is the blue-yellow channel, and finally the black-white channel, making it the luminance channel. Therefore, the eye the red-green value is more visible than the others.

With respect to the colors, red, orange, yellow, green, blue, indigo, and violet, you cannot see the light in these colors that I use because they are not being determined by eyesight. As I said before, light is not the same to the ear. It may help if you imagine the sound of a penny dropping. You probably "see" a falling brown coin with Lincoln's picture on it. The exact distance it falls is unknown if you cannot see it, but the sound is still very distinct in the mind.

Similarly, if you hear a nail being driven into a board, you may imagine that nail is silver as many nails are that color. Nails come in different sizes, yet they are virtually always the same shape. If you put together a puzzle, you use pieces of different shapes, but they are typically all about the same size. A collection of rocks, on the other hand, usually includes specimens of different colors, shapes, sizes, and forms. It is the same with voices. They have many similarities that are useful for comparison, but are all very different, too.

Chapter Three:

HOW THE COLORS ARE MADE UP IN THE SOUND OF THE VOICE

Color has three parts to it: the hue, the value, and the density. Coupled with their lightness or darkness, the different color shades, there are actually many possible colors within any one color. The three primary colors are blue, red, and yellow, and sometimes white is considered a primary color (it is also referred to as a neutral). Green is a secondary color, composed of blue and yellow, two of the primary colors. When you mix a primary with a secondary color you get what is called a tertiary color. Yellow-orange and blue-purple are tertiary colors.

Everything I've spoken of up to now contributes to the sound of a voice. A voice has wave, shape, and form to it. My way of looking at the hue, value, and the density is likely different than the way you, being a sighted person, understand it—if you think about it at all. You may know that hue, value, and density make up color, but not sound, and you probably have not ever thought of the color of a voice. When you hear a voice, however, it has a color with all three color attributes. Incidentally, a voice's colors do not have anything to do with the color of the skin of the person speaking, only the voice itself. There are silver voices here and half way across the world from us. The darkest voice I ever heard was Darth Vader's voice in the *Star Wars* film. It was black, but not because James Earl Jones is African-American. Rather, it was due to its hue, density, and value. Interestingly, it was black only when he portrayed Darth Vader. When Jones is not Vader, his voice is a very deep blue.

Every voice has its own unique sound of colors. We know orange is the true color of orange because the fruit, orange, is orange. It could just as well be red. The sound of the voice relates to our recollections of the things in our past, things that continue to appear as images in the mind. For example, if you hear wind chimes, your mind may immediately see a particular wind chime that your best friend once owned. This is because they are familiar and have become a mental reference.

Sound waves to the ears can be loud or soft in value, hue, and density, depending how far they have traveled, for each person focuses on sounds differently. Certain sounds hit fourteen different locations in the pinna. The pinna is the visible part of the ear, also called the auricle. The higher a sound the more it is focused in the middle of the pinna. A yellow voice is directed toward the middle, but a blue-black voice is farther on the other side of the pinna, because of how low it is.

Starting with the middle is a yellow voice in the first location in the pinna. This is the highest sound can go in color. The best way that I can describe this is to compare it to a dart board. Look on each side of the bull's-eye. Imagine the yellow sound is a circle starting with lightest shade you can visualize. The more you go outward on the dart board, the darker yellow becomes. A male's and a female's yellow voices are found in different places on the dart board. The male voice is darker yellow and the female voice lighter. But on the dart board, this can go with any color.

The second location is gold. There are many shades of those colors as well. After gold, the third in line is orange. The fourth is red, the fifth pink, sixth purple, and seventh blue. Then comes turquoise as eighth, ninth green and tan is tenth. Eleven is brown, twelve is black, thirteen gray, and finally, white comes in at fourteen. All sounds are created from white, which is similar to radio static or television snow. This sound is gray-white. It has an interesting sound like light white mixing with very dark gray, and a very dark white mixing with a light gray. Here is how it connects. Very deep dark gray is in the thirteenth location and connects with the twelfth location black, and the light gray in the thirteenth location connects with the fourteenth location white.

Let me explain further. From this chart, you can mix two locations together, like a blue-tan voice. A magenta color then will fit in the fourth and sixth red-purple locations. If the voice is forest, or lime, it will fit in the ninth green location. My mind can relate to forest green and lime green because it is something that I remember back when I could see. A cherry red voice is darker than a fire engine red. Some voices will fit in one location; others take two or three color locations, or sometimes four, depending on the mixtures of the colors of the hue and value. Take again a dartboard for one voice. If it is green-black, the center is black and around the bullseye is green. If it is black-green, vice versa. If the center is pink and yellow surrounds the bullseye, it will make a yellow-pink. If someone has magenta in the center, ocean-blue is around it. If magenta is on the outside, it's auburn in the middle. The color of your voice is not good or bad. Your sound is your voice color, and your voice color is your sound, the sound of your color.

Chapter Four:
COLOR LAYERS OF SOUND
AND THE SHAPE OF A VOICE

As I have explained, there are three main components of color and, likewise, three main parts of the colors of voices. It helps to consider each part separately:

1. The Hue

The hue is home base for the regular voice. It has a fixed color to it that does not change. The sounds you make when you speak go in and out through the hue, as well as through the material and nature elements of the voice. I will explain the nature and material elements later. The hue is located in the center of the voice and is shaped somewhat like a triangle, except that it lacks the bottom line. On each side of the slanted lateral lines, imagine a square shape, but don't include the top lines of the squares. This is what I am talking about when I refer to the shape of a voice, by its sound. The shape is always unique in itself. I will refer to the hue as a triangle. So it will be the "triangle hue".

The second layer of the hue has a picture of what a person likes, like a guitar, and even has a word that describes him or her, such as charisma. You find an individual's personality in the color of their voice. This is the key element to the voice. The colors that you like and I like are two different things.

Blue can be negative or positive. The negative side is like a frosty pale blue, like in the winter months when you look through a frosted window at the sky. The positive blue is easy going. Just like I said, someone may like cold weather, and some don't. Someone told me that they do not like the color blue, makes him think of being sad. For me, the positive blue is like the sky, or the blue ocean. Negative blue is cold weather, (I hate cold weather). So for me, positive blue is ocean blue, as frosty blue is negative.

There is a positive and negative sound for each color in the personality of the voice. Yellow is very pleasing to the mind, very sunny and cheerful. Yellow is a warm color, but ugly mustard yellow is of course negative. For example, a lot of people like mustard, but of course some don't. In this case, this is a negative yellow mustard to me. So a negative yellow will hang out with other negative colors, or also for example, a sunny positive yellow will hang out with other positive colors. I am a positive blue-black voice, by this I like the blue ocean, and love listening to night sounds at night during the summer time, and this equals blue-black. The voice color is handed down from generation to generation; I will go in to this later. So for example, I will hang out with someone that has a blue positive voice, but dating, the female must have a red voice, I will go in to this later too.

I don't clash too well with negative personality colors. Someone that I don't get along with has a negative personality sounding voice, but they think they are positive, and you are negative, but you think you are positive. It takes all kinds to make a world.

Colors have a warm and cool feeling to them. Warm colors are red, pink, orange, gold, and yellow. Cool colors are green, blue, and purple. Neutral colors are black, white, gray, and brown; also, tan and silver. Mixed cool-warm colors are turquoise, lavender, and magenta. All the pastel colors, pale soft colors or vibrant colors have to do with brightness, as well as the rich deep dark colors. All colors have negative and positive voice energy personality sound. There is no in between, either negative or positive. The only negative voice in this book is the first voice study.

You might know someone that has a green personality sound in their voice, and you don't get along to well. Think of something green, that you do not like. For me, it is peas (Jolly Green Giant). When I was five years old, I got to know the kitchen very well, because I would not eat five peas on my plate at the dinner table, and to this very day I still don't like them. I do like the color olive green. The reason is because the olive branch symbolizes peace. I always relate to what I like or don't like by the color, even if it is in the same shade in the color (positive or negative). Positive is what I like (olive green) and negative (pea green) is what I do not like, but for someone else, it will be different, especially if they have a negative personality energy sounding voice. I do know the 2 colors, pea green, and olive green but the word that describes the color has a great impact of how I feel about the color.

2. The Value

This is the second layer, outside of the triangular hue. It has its own color, separate from the hue. It also has a shape to it. The shape for a male is square. Females have a circular shape. The square and the circle are not perfect by any means. This is called free-form. These are irregular shapes, something that we don't see every day like we see regular shapes with our eyesight.

   The value is the depth of the color of the voice, like the light and darkness. It has to do with the way the person thinks and their actions and reactions, how they feel about things, and the mood that they are in at any given time when they speak. Lying, smiling, and sadness show in the voice. With these emotions, the sound of the voice fluctuates. The sound of sadness is slower than happiness, which is literally upbeat. As I've said, *rhythm* is the key word.

   But through this lightness or darkness shows another thing that comes from the hue; it is like a covering element over the nature and material elements that does not change color. Some of these elements are shadows, glowing, shining, et cetera. Each person only has one of these. This element mixes well with the light and darkness in a voice, making it one whole sound, but not exactly. It is unique for each person.

The first half of a word in a sentence emits a nature element similar to a river, rocks, the wind, or fire, a thing that is not man-made. Everyone has his or her own nature element. In a voice study I will refer to later, the nature element is fire. At the end of that word can be heard the sound of a material element, which is an object, something like a door, man-made. It reveals the things the speaker likes to do, such as watching movies. If that is indeed the case, the material element might be a DVD or blue ray disc. Everyone has their own material element. In the first of my voice studies, which I present later, the material element is a diamond, like a diamond ring or necklace. The nature and material elements do not interfere with the color of the voice. I picture in my mind what the person likes to do.

3. The Density

Density rests outside the sounds and shapes of the voice. It is white; all voices are based on it. It is what makes up the sound and shape of the voice. This is where your true self lies and your secrets, the things you keep to yourself, including the positive or negative perceptions you have of what others think of you and how you feel about yourself. Density might reveal a healthy ego or low self esteem. Its sound arises very, very quickly, when a person swallows or takes a breath while talking. A second of silence, too, affects density.

At this point it is important that I clarify more about the hue, value, and density in different situations. Let's say, for example, that there is a person that you do not know very well, but see often, perhaps briefly every day or so, like a fellow student in one of your classes, or a co-worker. This person cannot speak English very well. I had a friend like this in college and there was also another student from the same country. The two of them spoke their native language to each other, and although I didn't know the words, the same color tone from my friend's voice still was still apparent to me. Even now if he came up to me and started speaking in his native tongue, I would know him by his color.

To reiterate, the hue is always the same. The density reveals the state of mind, negative or positive. The value shows how a person feels at the time he is speaking, physically. Does he or she have a headache? Has he or she suffered a breakup with a boyfriend or a girlfriend? These things are evident in the sound, how quickly it travels back and forth in the value. The feeling in your voice you cannot hide, especially from a person who knows you well.

If a particular feeling comes to you when your friend speaks to you, this is called "reversed feelings." If you are speaking over a telephone, you can often pick up signals that something significant is affecting your friend. For example, his breathing may be slower, which is an indication of sadness (unless he is crying).

Chapter Five:
SENTENCES AND WORDS
AND MUSIC NOTES

1. Activator

Because a person is breathing while speaking, you hear breaks and pauses with their air intake and outflow. The frequency and duration of these breaks varies by person and in relation to their heart's rate. The Activator is apparent within the first few sentences one speaks and influences their density. Their color is always constant throughout the sentence or sentences, along with the value, nature, material, that connects together well. While taking a breath, a quick second of silence breaks the string in the color and in the sound or silence of the voice. Remember, the density is the white sound or silence to the voice.

When reading from a book, it occurs always after one sentence. When your voice sounds out a B, and a P, or the letter T, you halt your airstream. When the air comes back out, it will make varying degrees of sharpness in a sound. To say a V or a J, the airstream causes vibration. Each letter has its own air path of colors, too, but they are not apparent or clear until the sound goes through their value.

2. Amplifier

Your mouth, how wide you open it, causes your lips to make different shapes like wide open, closed, pursed, or stretched, and they all create different sounds. The Amplifier works very closely with the value and with the light and the dark, the brightness and the dullness. It controls how loudly you talk and the raising or lowering of your voice. This is the value of the voice.

When making the sound "ah" as in ostrich, you lower your jaw and your tongue. Amplification also depends how much the jaws are open.

3. Resonator

This has to do with the mouth and sinus cavities. This is the way your mouth is shaped and the passageway through which the voice resonates coming out of the mouth. How wide you open your mouth causes your lips to make different shapes like wide open, closed, pursed, or stretched, and they all create different resonance. When making the sound "ah" as in ostrich, you lower your jaw and tongue. Amplification and resonance depend on how wide the jaws are open. When sounding out consonants, the sound is affected by various movements of the tongue and lips. To sound out a vowel sound, such as "ee" as in three, the tongue moves toward the front of your palate, which widens the pharyngeal cavity; this also raises the larynx slightly. The throat and sinuses affect your talking voice. There is pressure on the color tone if your throat is sore or your sinuses congested. This will affect the resonance of your voice. You voice has less energy and is slower. A voice in any kind of pain is uneven.

The teeth also affect the voice. When you have a tooth pulled or have dentures, it will affect your voice.

Smoking changes the voice, too, especially with respect to breathing, the Activator. It affects the value, but the hue stays the same. Smoking makes a voice darker, but not unattractive. It actually gives it a wondering tone in my opinion.

There are three main levels to the voice:
        a. Down
        b. Regular
        c. Upper

These levels differ from person to person. A voice can go two steps up from its home base, but only the value changes. Rhythm is again the key word. When the voice comes out in a slower rhythm or a faster rhythm, you know something is up.

The first level is the scream, the farthest the voice can go—and the loudest. It is difficult to say words while screaming. A scream has gold in it, almost yellow. In fact, a scream for everybody is yellow. Yellow, to me, is the top color, the brightest color you can see, except for white, which is not applicable to voice level. Like a traffic light, yellow means beware, pay attention, danger is near, or it indicates surprise.

Below screaming is the level of yelling. Yelling uses your regular voice, except the volume from the value very quickly into the hue and out. Within the yelling range fits the crying voice you hear between sobs. These too have a yellow sound, but crying is a paler yellow than screaming. If someone talks between tears however, the voice is shaky, almost like being underwater, but the color does not change.

Below yelling, is the angry voice. The volume is down a little, but the voice is a full step above the regular voice. I think of red, like danger on the way or a red stop sign, but the voice does not show it. Also, below the yelling, you find the level that is used when you are excited or amazed. It uses less volume, but is much brighter by a half-step to a full step, depending on the situation. This is evident within the value and in how quickly the voice goes in and out of the hue. The nature and material elements are still there in the voice in the very note where this voice starts in the regular voice, and where it jumps up, by half a step or a full step. However, the color of the hue stays the same and whatever is said comes back down to the regular voice. Below the happy voice is the regular home base voice. The next level down is the moaning sound like one makes when in pain, physically or mentally. This is the same tone that your voice is tuned to, but the volume is a lot softer. This is very interesting because it is your regular voice, but without words.

In a whisper, the hue true color is formed, plus in the value it is very soft, but the nature and material elements are still there, for whatever is said.

Starting down from the regular voice is the voice that reveals sadness or feeling "under the weather." A headache and stress meet at the same level, but usually a pain sound is with the headache. You cannot tell when a person has a cold or a sore throat. It depends how well you know the person. But the voice will either be above or below the home base voice.

For example, when you travel on an airplane, the middle ear gets stopped up. The middle ear is like an air pocket that does not like changes in air pressure. Chewing gum, yawning, or swallowing can offer relief. The popping sound that you hear after doing these things is actually from an air bubble that comes from the back of your nose. It travels through the Eustachian tube, which connects the back of the nose to the middle ear. I will explain this later on. When someone is stressed or in pain, their words come out slower. The next level has to do with being worn out. When tired, often very late at night, my voice slows down. Below that is the sound of being "not happy" to see you. At the bottom is sadness.

The words you say have their own colors, which reside within the material and nature elements. This is the final level to the material and nature elements. Words do not cancel out the voice's essential color, or the material and nature elements. The color of the words is in the first layer of the hue. In singing, each note you sing has a color of its own, too; so, we get the hue of the voice, the colors of the words, and the colors of the notes. Also, different rhythms are at work simultaneously. You have just the talking rhythm, and the singing rhythm voice. The singing voice must flow with the music and the notes while the talking rhythm must follow words.

For example, a reddish pink voice sings a D above middle C.

The note is black in sound. If the word sung is "table," I picture a table that is brown, light and dark-striped, because in my childhood there was such a table in the kitchen I remember best. Not all tables are brown in color, of course, but that is the first table I remember, so it affects the word color. The old saying that a picture has a thousand words comes to bear here. Every image we can imagine is rooted in our memories, which conjure up images. Every image means something different to each of us.

Letters alone have color. In the above example, the whole word "table" is brown, but when you spell it out, each letter has its own color. T is gray, A is white, B is brown, and L is a deeper white than A— with a touch of gray in it. E is white as the snow (see chart below). The shapes of these letters are the typical shapes of letters as you know them. But when you hear the letters in color, it is called synesthesia.

This is the way I see the alphabet. You may want to mark this page because I will be referring to this list later.

List of Letters and Music Notes in Colors

A - white
A sharp - very light yellow
B - brown
C - gold
C sharp - tan
D - black
D sharp - pale orange
E - white as snow, with a splash of light green in it, but on piano it is blue
F - off-green, in between green and black
F sharp - is silver
G - mint green,
G sharp - red,
H - gold
I - off-black
J - red
K - black off white
L - middle white

M - dark brown as a dark wooden door
N - off-gold
O - mediocre white
P - gold-orange
Q - silver-gray
R - red, like cellophane paper
S - off-white with a touch of gray
T - gray-black
U - cloudy gray
V - emerald green
W - black as midnight
X - off-green, with different colors of green running through it
Y - yellow-brown
Z - gray-black, with a hint of white wandering through it

In the word "blue," you actually imagine the color blue, lighter or darker, depending on your own concept of it, but the letters in this word each carry their own colors and affect the meaning. In the word "and," the colors are white, gold, and black. The acronym "D.N.A." is actually the reverse: black, gold, and white. The "i" is silent in the word "piece," but it still resides within the word. However, verbally it does not show up at all.

The name Shawn sounds green to me but may have a yellow-gold voice. Cathy sound red to me, but she might have a purple-red voice. The colors are not good or bad. The narrowness, width, deepness, and length give shape to the letter sounds and the syntax and diction.

With synesthesia, even numbers have their own colors. The following list represents my mind seeing numbers.

Number chart

0. mediocre white
1. Shadowy black
2. Gray-white
3. Glowing in the light, but is dark red
4. Gold that stands out
5. Cool black
6. Army green, deep green
7. Off-gold
8. Black as midnight
9. Shadowy fading gold that stands off by itself
10. Mediocre blue
11. Black as black can go
12. Concrete gray

Chapter Six:
BACKGROUND COLORS OF MOODS AND FEELINGS

This brings up the background of my mind colors. The background colors are my feelings and moods. Someone asked what colors I saw as a sort of background inside my head. "Is it like seeing outer space and seeing spaceships flying around, and white stars shining bright?" No, not at all. My mind colors pretty much match my facial expressions.

Here are the background colors I do see. When I am happy, or hyper, the background is red. When sad or lonely it's blue. When feeling mediocre, purple. When the color is magenta, I'm feeling loved. When I'm scared, or surprised it's orange. When confused, or being sidetracked, it is gray. When in pain, or at peace it's white. When angry or upset, black. When excited, or curious, it is the color gold. And brown when I feel discouraged or burnt out. I see lime green when I encounter something that I have not experienced or not familiar with, something new. Emerald green when I'm panicked or dreading doing something. When embarrassed, it is mustard yellow, but when I am tired, canary yellow. When I feel under the weather or feel awful, it is the color baby blue. Pink, when feeling like a clown, or being immature. When puzzled about something, or being bored, it is the color tan. When the "color" is clear, I am concentrating, or focused. When I feel awkward, aqua, and when having fun, it is my favorite color -- silver.

This *does not* cancel out the colors of voices, music, numbers, letters, words, and name colors. Picture a domino, with the dividing line that creates two sections, a number on top, and a number on the bottom. A voice that sounds yellow-pink says the word tired in gray-black; I will picture gray-black on the top section and yellow-pink below. In the background, silver will surround the other colors (but *will not* mix them up or together). Remember, silver is the color I see when I am having fun (see chart). Each word will change colors in seconds. For example, "I am so tired." With the yellow-pink voice, I will see the word "I" as off-black with yellow-pink below and the background will be silver. The next word "am" sounds orange-red, below is yellow-pink, and silver is in the background, and finally the word tired is gray-black. So "I am tired" will be off-black with yellow-pink, and silver in the background then orange-red with yellow-pink, and silver in the background, and finally gray-black, with yellow-pink and silver in the background.

Letters and numbers also go above the voice color. So if someone says in their sky blue-magenta voice, "AK-47," I will see white, sky blue-magenta, with aqua in the background (See chart -- Aqua is awkward). Keep on visualizing a domino. A is the color white. K is black off white, sky blue-magenta with aqua in the background. Four (4) is gold that stands out, with sky blue-magenta and aqua background. Finally, I will see seven (7) off-gold, sky blue-magenta with aqua background. After "AK-47" is said, I visualize a machine gun or something like it that I remember from my childhood, a picture of some kind, or from television. I visualize these things by what the voice is saying, not the voice itself. I hardly focus, on the voice color, because it is pretty much constant through the whole entire sentence.

I have noticed that in a restaurant setting, the background noises are in gold, even the music and even if I barely can hear it. Visualize a traffic light. From top to bottom, gold, blue (stands for the word "what"), with voice color blue-black on the bottom and a purple background (mediocre). So the colors will be gold, blue, blue-black, and purple background.

When sitting alone in a restaurant, I pay more attention to the music, and listen to other conversations while I sit silently. I can only focus only on one thing, or just one level, and that is mostly the music playing, or hearing someone with their voice color say a word or two, that stands out to me. After hearing this person talking, my mind will go back to the music. My mind can go from level to level, with no problem, but remember, I can only focus on one thing at a time. Here is the way my mind sees things in a situation in a restaurant setting: Picture a house with a basement, a main floor, an upstairs, and an attic. From top to bottom, gold is on top (remember the background noise). Then the song color, and red (word color); the word is "right." Voice color will be the color orange-red in the basement with a blue background (sad). Colors will be gold, song color, red, orange-red, and a blue background. I will explain Music Tone Colors later.

Chapter Seven:
OUTLINE OF A VOICE STUDY

Try to recall the sound of a voice you know very well, for example, Harrison Ford or Miley Cyrus. This could be anybody's voice. I will describe the color tone in the voice using one of my best voice studies in my collection.

To understand the way the voice is put together in one sound, remember that it consists of three layers. When I talk about the hue, this is the third layer in the center of the voice. Value is in the second layer the lightness and darkness of the mood of the person's voice. Finally, density is the third layer and measures the thickness and heaviness of the voice. This is where your regular voice starts up from at the start of the sentence and ends at the end of the sentence or when you are done talking. It takes all three parts, hue, value, and density to make up the sound of the voice. Just like a color needs all three attributes to make that unique color.

Voice Study #1
This voice has a fire, a diamond; it's a shiny blue voice. It is not tuned to E on the chart "A List of Letters and Music Notes in Colors". There are nature and material elements in the voice. The fire is the nature element. The material element is the diamond. The diamond, in this case, is like a jewelry piece, perhaps a necklace, bracelet, or ring. Sometimes it takes a while to determine these things, but I know this person pretty well.

The fire element shows up at the start of each word she says. If she said, "how are you?" —at the start of each word "how," "are," "you," all begin with the fire element.

The material element, diamond, comes in on the last part of the words, "how are you."

The fire and diamond can be light or dark, depending on her mood or feelings. When excited, her voice will go up half a step, but it does not lose the fire and the diamond element to it. If sad, her voice drops half a step lower. When a person is sad, the sounds move more slowly through the voice. The shiny blue appears over the nature and material parts of the voice, but the shiny blue always maintains its color.

When you speak, your voice starts out in the density, which I will get back to later. The nature and material parts are formed in the value. The value can have its own color, too. This particular voice is the color blue. Its value shape is a circle with the sides dented in.

The triangle hue that is in the center of this voice has its own color, too. I found it interesting that the value and the hue are almost the same color blue in this voice. The hue is darker than the value though. The hue always stays this color while the value changes because of mood and feelings. This shows aspects of very, very light gray to the voice. The hue or home base of the voice is in the center of the voice. How did I decide the color blue for her voice? It is pale blue like looking out the winter window covered in frost. In the second layer of the hue where there is a word and a picture to describe this individual, the word is sanguine. The picture is a book because she loves to study.

This brings me to the first layer, the density. Remember, no matter whom the person is, the density is always white. The density has no shape. All sound starts with it and dies out with it. The positives and negatives about how one feels about himself or herself and others are located here, too. The voice in this case is negative. It contains love and hate qualities in the background, in the way it comes across. I have seen this person talk to others and that certain quality, which is unique to her, is still there. This quality can really stand out, depending on what kind of mood she is in.

The Way the Voice Study Sounds within the Colors

With the "snapshot" I have just set up for you, I will now describe how the sound gets to its source and retreats back away from the center in the triangle hue. The start of her sentences begins in the density, the nature element, which is fire in this study, and goes into the blue (value) dented circle. This activates the shape of the dented circle and also goes into the darker blue hue.

Once the nature element, fire, reaches the hue, it completes the shape of the hue and the value shape at once, each having its own boundaries in its color. At once, the two shapes become visible in a sentence. Remember, at the first part of the word is the nature element, fire, and at the last part is the material element, diamond. The fire and diamond keep bouncing back and forth. The darker blue hue and the changing color blue value do not affect the colors at all. This happens so fast, it is almost impossible to keep up with it. The extra element that covers the nature and material elements is present. Remember this is shiny blue in this voice study.

In the hue triangle, the different colors of her words are apparent at the same time. The value, the light, and the darkness of the color blue change when she is excited or sad. When a word or sentence is uttered, by its last sound, the material element, diamond, goes back out and into the white density. The density is evident in a swallow or deep breath, or in a moment of silence.

In all the voice studies I have conducted, the colors of the hues and the colors of the values are very similar. One guy had a blue-black voice but was more on the black side. We were about the same age, and the frequency note was the same but looked different than I did. He had a totally different childhood. I will explain more about this in the section "Voice Frequencies." In one case, a female friend's value is the color brown, but her hue is the color purple. Interestingly, the sound starts off very wide in the color brown, and when the sound gets close to the center of her voice, where the purple picks up, it becomes narrow, but when the sound bounces back out it becomes wide again in the color brown, and this happens every single time, making her voice the most unique indeed. Remember what I said before about every color having shape -- narrow, wide, and deep. In the prettiest voice case study I have, the voice starts off in purple, then turns to sky blue in the value and the center hue is pink. Coming back out, the color is fire engine red in the value and goes back in to purple.

Another Voice Study

I will now do another voice study without going into all of the details. To begin, this voice is a male. He produces a sound wave in color that is the ocean, a radio, and a glowing brown-tan voice, not tuned to B on the chart "A List of Letters and Music Notes in Colors". The triangle hue is very well tan; the value is off-brown square, and the density is, of course, white. The value has the shape of a square. It is not exactly square shaped though. The best way I can describe it is to take a square and cut off the four corners, which makes it an octagon in shape. The lines do not match. This is in the value of the color and where the regular voice comes into the off-brown value square.

The ocean is the nature element, but is not activated until it is formed in the off-brown value square and the radio, the material element that brings the sound back out. This radio element is like static, trying to get the station in better. All voices have the same format, like the structure of a sentence, and the material and the nature element comes in and goes out of it. The element that covers the nature and material elements is a glowing gold color, which blends into the off-brown color value.

Outside of the off-brown square value is the density, which carries the white sound over to the brown square, but the white is still present when it goes into the tan hue. These two colors -- brown and tan -- were the colors of my favorite pair of leather Nike shoes while growing up. I got the shoes after I lost my eye sight but I could still visualize in my head what the shoes looked like. The Nikes fit this voice perfectly because the shoe was brown leather, and right down the middle was a strip of swirl tan leather, and on the bottom were white soles. I remember leather things from when I had my eye sight, like jackets or briefcases. I have another friend who has the same color tones, but a different shade of brown and tan. His voice is browner and it showed up in his voice more because he talked a lot faster, and you don't get to hear much tan. These two voices have different backgrounds. One was in the Marines, and the other did not serve in the armed forces and is from my generation.

In the second layer in the hue, the center of the voice is a picture that I get of a car. This is interesting because when I say the word "car," I might see in my mind either one or another image. This is because a word can bring up more than one image sometimes. For instance, you may remember the last car you saw earlier in a day, or the first car that you ever saw as a child.

The mind always holds an image to remind itself of a word. A man dressed in a white coat with a stethoscope around his neck is, of course, a doctor. In the voice, the image picture does not work as well as this. I might see a tree, but it could be blue or purple with orange and red leaves on it.

The word in the second layer of the hue is "tenacious." Remember, this is where the true self, the personality is found.

Again, the density is where your true self resides, including your negatives and positives. This particular voice is neither positive nor negative; it is in-between. The subject gets along with others, but there is also something serious in his density that tells a different story.

Voice Frequencies
With music notes, as the scales going up, the colors get brighter, and lighter. With the octaves below, they get dull and darker. The colors do not change just the darkness, lightness, dullness and brightness.

To understand the frequency notes on the piano, following is a chart of all the A's, where the human voice ranges are in pitch or sound.

A 440 is the one most musicians talk about

An octave below C4 then A is 220

C4, or middle C, then A is 440

C5 octave then A is 880

C2 then A is 110

If your voice is above middle C, take the number note and multiply it by 2 or 3. If it is *below* middle C *divide* it by 2 or 3. While your speaking voice fits in this range, your singing doesn't. You might need a musician friend to help you figure out your home base singing note; that is, the note your singing voice is tuned to. To find your home base singing note, say a word, and hold it, and find the note on the piano that matches it. My note is A octave below middle C or C4, white. The frequency is then 110, but my voice color is blue-black. While another male voice has the same frequency, he might have a green-blue voice. Chart starting with middle C, or C4.

C - 262
C sharp - 277
D - 294
D sharp - 311
E - 330
F - 349
F sharp - 370
G - 392
G sharp - 415
A - 440
A sharp - 466
B - 494

Music Tone Colors

I love to experiment with different songs. I thought it would be cool to put a song in a different music style. One day I thought, instead of playing "Stand By Me" in its original rock-and-roll style, why not try making it sound country? I answered my own question later on that day. I walked into a gas station and the radio was set to a country music station. I listened to "Stand by Me" in a country style of music. The color of the song had a red feel to it, but the original has a silver feeling to it. Interestingly enough, these are my favorite colors. However, my favorite red is a very deep red and the country song had more of a very light red feel. But I like any color of silver.

Remember, this is not in G sharp, or in F sharp (see section "A List of Letters and Music Notes in Colors"). The original "Stand By Me" is chrome silver to me. This is not breaking down the song at all, this is the feeling I get when listening to both of these songs. There are not too many songs that I can feel like this without paying attention to the chords and melody.

I love to listen to re-mixes of songs and see how different they sound from their originals. Of course, how you feel and the mood you are in determines what you listen too. I especially love a particular remix of "American Woman" by Lenny Kravitz because it is nice and slow. However, when the Guess Who plays this song, it's bouncy. I feel like listening to one or the other, depending on my mind color. If happy (red), it is the Guess Who, if sad (blue) Lenny Kravitz. With the Kravitz remix, I see the music colors black-red, and with the Guess Who I see red, white, and blue.

I've listened to "Leaving On a Jet Plane" on a karaoke machine and found it to be very slow. At the nursing home where I do music therapy sessions, I play this song fast on my guitar. I play upbeat like Frank Sinatra sings it. When listening to the Peter, Paul, and Mary version, I see the color in different shades of browns and tans intertwining together. With the Sinatra version, I see blue and white. It is like I can see a white jet "now silver," but these are the things I remember in the 1970's, a jet in the clear blue sky. John Denver's version of "Leaving On a Jet Plane" sounds gold and green. Green is the sound of Denver's singing voice and the music is gold. It gives you a mellow feel, just like Peter, Paul, and Mary does. The remix of the song done by a group called Slightly Stoopid gives me a traveling feel, a time-to-hit-the-road feel, and I see the colors red and gold because of the tropical beat, a different shade of gold than Denver's version. Slightly Stoopid's version has a real shining gold. Often I love a song, but wish it had a different singer. To me, it's very important that the music fit the singer's voice. It is the color tone of the music and the color feelings of the singer that are most pleasing to the mind. You might like of one remix more than the other, which is fine of course because what I like and what you like is naturally different.

The singer Olivia Newton-John has a blue-silver talking voice. But when she sings "Magic" I see light silver and red with the words, and the music is gold and black. The word magic sounds green, because of its width and narrowness. Remember the traffic light to visualize this. The music is at the top, the singing voice comes in the middle, and the colors of the words come in at the bottom. The silver I see in the song is Olivia's singing voice, red being the echo after each word she says blending in with the music. Her singing voice is silver but not tuned to F sharp (see "A List of Letters and Music Notes in Colors").

John Lennon has a green voice, but when he sings "Imagine," his singing voice is green-gold. The song sounds gold-white, pure and innocent, with a touch of green in it. (Lennon's green voice has nothing to do with the key of G, but maybe he did like this key, I don't know.)

Frank Sinatra's singing technique is my favorite. He sings above the given notes. At least this is what I have been told, and it does sound like that to me. His singing voice is blue-white but his talking voice is medium blue. Sometimes I have a hard time determining this, especially if it is a singer that I don't listen to. For other songs, the words tell you what you should see in your mind. For example, with "Bridge Over Troubled Water" I can picture what the words are saying. I can see a bridge with blue water below it. Also, with "The Long and Winding Road" (The Beatles) I can see a road with lots of turns, and the song itself I see as glowing white with shiny gold vocals. Songs that have objects, or talk about a place, I can picture the object or place in my mind. For songs like "Don't Stop" by Fleetwood Mac, the colors are red, yellow, and orange, or the song "You Light Up My Life" by Debbie Boone, is gold and red. I am more likely to think about how it relates to my life. All songs have their meanings and memories, and yes any time I hear the song "Can't Fight This Feeling" by REO Speedwagon, I always think of the first girl I danced with back in seventh grade. I have not talked to her in about ten years.

A lot of bands like ZZ TOP, and The Who have a unique sound. You can always tell it's their music. In all music, the drums are the backbone of the song. When I hear the drums, I picture white, black, and gold. The white part is the snare drum, the black is the bass drum, and the gold is the cymbal, the closed or open hi-hat. The cymbal and the hi-hat have the same color tones to me. A tom-tom drum I hear in a darker white sound than the snare drum. I remember seeing a drum set back in the 1970's, and I remember the snare drum was the color white, and so were the tom-toms. The cymbal and the hi-hat are the color gold. I know a bass drum is not black, but I think of it as the opposite is white because you always need the bass drum to come in right after the snare drum. Between black and white, I think gold. Again, this has nothing to do with the key of C or A (see "A List of Letters and Music Notes in Colors").

For a bass guitar, I picture the notes being black. I believe this is how low the bass guitar notes can go. Also, plucking it with your fingers, gives it this sound. When I hear a heavy metal lead guitar part, I can see the color silver, mainly because of the loudness. This is not in F sharp (see "A List of Letters and Music Notes in Colors"). Because it is so fast I cannot tell the notes, but if the lead guitar part was in a classic rock song, I can figure it out. Whatever comes above the drums, like a rhythm guitar, and piano, and so on, have their own color, but it can be any color at all, not like the drum set. When I hear a trumpet being played alone, I picture the color gold, no matter what note is being played. It has nothing to do with middle C. If the note is a D, I see a gold-black sound, but the gold is stronger than the D, no matter how hard the note is being played. I also think of gold when I hear a saxophone being played alone but a different lighter gold than the trumpet. When hearing D on the sax, I hear gold-black, but like the trumpet, gold is stronger. There are different ranges of the sax, such as tenor, or alto, but they have their light and darkness of the gold sound to me. With a flute, no matter what note is being played, I picture white. I believe this is how high the notes can go, nothing to do with the key of A. Also, a recorder sounds white; it sounds very peaceful. Always the first song you learn on the recorder is "Hot Cross Buns." After that semester of college, I was so sick of hearing that song, I thought I could never listen to it again. I believe instruments that sound gold or white are because they are wind instruments. I am familiar with the trumpet and sax, and the recorder because I played them both in college classes. A violin on the other hand, has a green sound when being played alone. This is nothing to do with G. I believe this is because of playing the instrument with a bow. Like the note D again, I see the green-black sound of the note, but green is stronger, no matter how hard it is being played. A bagpipe also has a green sound probably because it should be outside with the trees. I believe this is how loud it can get. When playing A flat or G sharp, the color is red, but it sounds red-green to me, with green still being stronger.

Back in the day, I played the violin and the bagpipes. All these instruments sound different with other instruments being played. Every instrument has its own shape and size, and each instrument is unique in itself. With a piano and guitar, you can play more than one note, so there is a combination of colors. I have noticed when you play a C chord, C-E-G, it does still have the gold sound, but if you played E-G-C, it is blue-gold since E is the bottom note and E sounds blue to me. But if you played G-C-E, it is green-gold, because G is the bottom note, and G sounds green. The bottom note influences the chord, but the bottom note you hear more than the others.

Chapter Eight:
SINGING VOICE

I find it very interesting that when listening to someone sing all the notes up and down the scale in their regular tone voice, the color hue is still the same, even when on a different note than the one the voice is tuned to.

You can strain the singing voice and the regular voice by singing too loud and when you don't take care of the voice. Water and lemon juice do wonders for a strained voice. The value has a great deal of influence on the singing voice. Even if the voice is flat, everybody knows exactly what the real tune note should be because of the value.

In the scale, there are seven notes. Once, in a Music class, my professor sang from C to D with the piano. In between, there were 12 other notes. C sharp, or D flat are each just one note in that 12. In the 8 notes from C to high C, if all the notes were added, there would be 72 notes in the scale. Although there are some specially-built pianos that have 96 notes in a scale. One of the leading composers in the 1930's and 1940's, Julian Carrillo, built this kind of piano. I have never seen one, but would love to play it.

I do not know if you have noticed, but I know this from experience, that singing "er", and words that end with a T or D sound different in a regular talking voice. Also, if you say words with the P sound, those words will be louder than the other words. This is especially significant in the microphone. You have to adjust the distance you position it farther away from your mouth when you speak words that begin with these letters or sounds.

I said before that the hue color never changes, but the value and density do, and the way the sound travels through its course. This is true until a girl begins singing in her head voice or a guy goes into his falsetto voice. Then, the hue changes.

When a choir sings, all the females singing together make a single white sound while singing the same note. An all male choir sounds midnight-black. Together they make a gold sound like when you pour a soda beverage into a glass and the fizz slowly goes down. To me it is the color gold.

When you wake up every morning, your voice is not warmed up or fully awake. The value and density are different because the voice is moving slower and not totally in tune yet. From singing myself, I find it is best usually to sing at the end of the day when my voice is completely warmed up from talking all day. Then I can hit the notes correctly.

Just one person singing makes an interesting two color tone. The middle C on the piano sounds gold to me too, although this is not my favorite color (silver is, and that is F sharp below middle C). A red voice of a girl singing middle C will have a density and value that is gold. Her regular red voice is still there in the middle. There is not an ugly note on the piano and when someone is playing and the singing is good, all the colors flow nicely together.

It's remarkable that, if a girl's voice is tuned to E and is red, E on the piano is white, but the format that I explained earlier can come out sounding red with brightness or dullness, lightness and darkness, etc.

Songs alone, have their own color. The singer adds to a song and it will sound like music if done well. Singers sing with feeling and, of course, their eyes and facial expressions send out their own messages. Listening to a radio though, you have to go by sound alone. Some say, when practicing singing, it helps your sound to look in a mirror. Another tip for a good singing voice is to keep the tip of your tongue below your teeth. To take care of the voice, place a warm, wet towel around your neck and do not speak for ten minutes after a long day. In the morning to have a clear sounding voice, gargle with warm water containing baking soda and salt (1/2 teaspoons of each).

Even your posture affects your voice. There are many singing styles, such as opera, which involves vibrato, to nearly yelling, like in rap and some rock n' roll. Some other things to remember are diaphragm support, breath support, and stomach support. My favorite vocal warm up before singing is the old saying "how now brown cow." To sing well, the key word should be relaxed to get the best sound.

Research has shown that most Americans speak lower than they sing. In Europe, the opposite is true. A Soprano's voice is at its prime when the singer is in the age range of 21-24 years of age. The bass voice's prime is around 30-32. The different parts of a choir are, of course, soprano, alto, tenor, and bass. There are also parts inside these parts, like the mezzo-soprano, the middle female voice. Then you have the coloratura, a soprano that sings ornamental passages in music. Contralto is a low female voice. The countertenor is the highest male voice, which is often a falsetto. Then comes the Baritone or middle male voice.

Above the falsetto and the head voice is the whistling voice. This actually involves whistling a song while singing it at the same time. Some sopranos and altos can do this if they have the proper voice training. Men can sometimes accomplish this, but nothing like women can do it. The reason is the whistling singing voice is above the soprano high C, or F, or G notes. When you whistle, your epiglottis closes down over the larynx, creating the smallest shape in the resonating chamber. This causes very little vibration through the anterior parts of the vocal cords. The shorter vibrations make the higher notes easier to achieve. Babies usually have no trouble reaching these whistling sounds, but doing so too much can create problems with their vocal cords later on in life.

As a final point, there is "perfect pitch" or "absolute pitch," the ability to play a note heard, without seeing it, and also to play it back with accuracy. One who has perfect pitch does not have better hearing. Rather, it is matter of the way his or her ear picks up on a note or music. Having this is sometimes a blessing and sometimes a curse. My ears are so sensitive that lots of times when I listen to opera, it sounds like the opera singer's voice can break glass. One day strangely enough I was "watching" Dr. Oz, and the segment was called "Extreme Myths Busted." The myth "a human voice or opera singer can break glass" obviously caught my attention. We have seen children (or have done this ourselves) getting their fingers wet and running them over an empty glass causing it to make an annoying humming sound. In the segment, it was said, this sound is created by the natural frequency of the glass. A singer sang that same frequency, and the glass shattered. The note needs to be at least 117 decibels for it to shatter. That can be hard on my ears.

Chapter Nine:

SITUATION OF COMMUNICATION OF A CONVERSATION FORMULA

Now I am going to look at the way a voice comes across to you. The light energy, in this case, is in the colors of the voice and the words and letters being said. "Quickness" refers to how large the room is and how loudly the words are spoken. Then, there is the color of the voice itself, the sender to the receiver (what is being communicated); and finally, a picture is formed in the mind of the communication process in conversation.

A person's regular voice is as follows:
Voice = sound energy times quickness; Loudness = harshness + pain over soreness

In the words being encoded by the receiver, it is:
Size and shape = shapes into sizes in words. This is to understand the sender.

So this means:
Color = width or length over wideness or narrowness.

So this is:
Echo = change in the color, fullness or lightness, which is the distance, traveled over the size of the word shapes

And this means:
Sound Energy = echo location over distance travel; Distance traveled = from point a. to b., sender to receiver.

And this means:
The form of the voice is the letter over more letters that make up a word. The letter color, with the other letters and the word colors over that, form a word picture in the mind.

For this to make more sense, location finally is the quickness in the speed, which determines how far the voice travels as it is being heard.

So this means:

Mood = mind color background to the other voice color, over gold, and the background sounds. Your mood is affected by the conversation with your friend, and the noises of the background sounds.

Gold background noises = flying colors of words from Point A, you, to point B, your friend, back to point A. These are all of course in words, using words.

Then in music:

A singer's voice = color tone of regular voice with color tones of notes over the instruments being played. The singer's voice is mixed with the tone of the instruments. The "strength" of one color over another will depend on which is more prominent, the voice or the instrument.

Two different colors of tones = the mixture of colors in one.

From my life experience, this is the way the voice travels and sounds to me. From talking to friends in person or on the telephone, one to one, this is the way the process works.

Chapter Ten:
STAGES OF LIFE
AND THE DEVELOPING
COMMUNICATION SKILLS

Now we are going to look at how the voice is developed through childhood to the teenage years. The color tone is present when the child is born, but of course the vocal sound does not come right away. The newborn does a lot of screaming and crying.

In Piaget's Four Stages of Cognitive Development, when a child is born and begins leaning words and responding to voices and sounds, the first voices they typically get to know are those of their parents. At two months of age, a child will fix its attention on a singer. At twelve to eighteen months, a baby starts to babble. Usually its first words are "Mom" or "Dad," or some variation of those words. At nineteen months, the little one starts to show rhythmic patterns in its vocal sounds, and from ages two to seven, he or she learns more words, can talk fast or slow, and sing words in songs. Also, the child's sentence structure becomes more developed. If a child is born deaf, the vibrations are very important because his or her focus must be on a person's lips moving in order to understand what is being said.

You will meet people that sound alike or very similar. Many people have the same beliefs, values, or densities evident in their voices, but they do not share the same color hues. At around age 17 or 18, after high school, the voice is fully developed, having a fixed shape and size, in addition to its unique color.

There are six different types of people on the face of the earth. There are four different categories that this fits in. Of course we can do most of these, and we are best at two of them. The six different types are:

1. reading, and writing
2. reading, and listening
3. reading, and talking
4. writing, and listening
5. writing, and talking
6. listening, and talking

For me, I am number 4. Of course, someone else will be number 1, or number 5.

Chapter Eleven:
OUTLINE OF THE VOCAL CORDS

What makes the color tone sound in the grown up years? The voice is made up of a larynx, also known as the voice box, which has more work to do than facilitating voice production. The larynx is also in charge of swallowing and breathing. When air goes through the vocal cords, it makes them vibrate and sound waves also move through the pharynx, which are affected by the nose and mouth. The amount of tension on the vocal folds, or vocal cords, determines the sound.

Vocal cords are made up of twin enfoldings of mucous membrane stretched horizontally across the larynx. They vibrate and control the amount of air being sent out from the lungs during phonation. The vocal cords are open during inhalation, but closed when you breathe. They vibrate when you talk or sing. They oscillate about 440 times per second when singing A above middle C. The voice's natural fundamental frequency is determined by the length, size, and tension of the vocal cords. For an adult male it is about 125 Hz; an adult female is about 210 Hz. Children are about 300 Hz. The lower the voice goes, the larger the folds—between 17 millimeters or 25 millimeters in length. For the female they stretch between 12.5 millimeters or 17.5 millimeters in length.

The vocal cords are white in color, but appear whiter in females. They are located between the epiglottises, which is a lid-like flap separating the windpipe from the esophagus, which is above the cords. Coupled with the different sizes, the cords create varied pitches and tones.

The false folds, also called the vestibular folds, are located above the vocal cords. They are a pair of thick folds of mucous membranes that protect the more delicate true vocal cords. False folds are only used in throat singing, in screaming, or in a grunt. They have a minimal role in normal phonation.

Below the cords is the trachea, which is more commonly referred to as the windpipe. The larynx is attached to the thyroid on the back side near the spinal cord and on the front side, beneath the chin, to the thyroid cartilage.

There are some common medical conditions of the vocal cords, such as nodules and polyps. A polyp is a soft, smooth lump composed mostly of blood and blood vessels. A nodule is similar, but tends to be more firm. Both are typically noncancerous and most often found in very young boys, teenage girls, and older women. It is believed that these conditions are caused by using the upper range of the voice too much because the vocal cords are not thick. Singers actually get this condition, too, especially those that sing in the higher ranges. For this reason, voice rest is recommended. There are also studies supporting that smoking and allergies cause polyps and nodules.

Laryngitis, inflammation of the vocal cords in the larynx, usually lasts about seven days and is not serious, most of the time. The symptoms are a weak, hoarse, gravelly voice with sore throat and fever, a dry cough, and sometimes tickling in the back of the throat and difficulty swallowing. A viral infection is the usual cause; however, even when the viral infection is gone, the laryngitis often lingers.

Occasionally, laryngitis is the result of a bacterial infection or strain. Strain can occur from overexertion of the voice, as when one cheers loudly for an extended time at a concert or sports game, or sings or talks loudly for a long period of time. Being in a smoky room or smoking yourself can also cause laryngitis. Cough drops are helpful in relieving the symptoms.

Chapter Twelve:
VOICE DISORDERS AND DISEASES AND OTHER CAUSES

Certain disorders of the voice manifest themselves in various ways. The first one I will talk about is Apraxia, which is characterized by difficulty saying what one wants to say correctly and consistently. This disorder is not due to the speech muscles, the muscles of the face, tongue, mouth or lips. There are actually two types of Apraxia: Acquired Apraxia of Speech and Developmental Apraxia of Speech.

Acquired Apraxia can affect anyone at whatever age, but appears mostly in adulthood after damage to the speech centers of the brain, such as may occur from stroke, head injury, tumor, and other sicknesses that attack the brain. When muscle weakness is affecting speech production, the disorder is Dysarthria (some refer to it more generally as language difficulties caused by damage to the nervous system). This may result in a condition called Aphasia. Aphasia can also be the result of a stroke, brain tumor, or severe injury, such as a gunshot wound.

Developmental Apraxia is a childhood condition; some children are born with it and it affects boys more than girls. Developmental Apraxia also goes by a few other names: Developmental Verbal Dyspraxia, Articulatory Apraxia, or Childhood Apraxia of Speech.

Spasmodic Dysphonia affects the voice quality making the voice break up produce a tight strained or strangled quality. It is a neurological voice disorder that causes the vocal cords to have involuntary spasms.

Stuttering is another voice disorder of unclear cause. It involves weakness and poor muscle coordination and the rate of language development may be a factor. Stuttering is characterized by unintentional repetitions of sounds, syllables, parts of a word, whole words, and/or complete phrases. It involves stretching out of sounds and syllables and also hesitation between words. Stutterers often speak in spurts, causing tense muscles in the jaw and mouth, and a loss of a sense of control.

Another voice disorder is vocal cord paralysis, a condition involving one or both of the vocal cords that do not open or close effectively. If one vocal cord does not work, the voice usually sounds hoarse or breathy. This is very common and ranges from mild to serious. In many cases, those affected swallow and cough often because food and liquids slip easily into their windpipes and their lungs because the paralyzed cord or cords remain open leaving the airway and lungs unprotected.

Vocal cord paralysis can result from head trauma, stroke, neck injury, lung or thyroid cancer, a tumor pressing on a nerve, or a viral infection. It can affect older people through neurologic conditions such as multiple sclerosis or Parkinson's disease.

Additionally, voice quality can show symptoms of loss of volume or pitch. One of the instruments used to diagnose this condition is an acoustic spectrograph, which measures voice frequency and clarity. Voice therapy is beneficial for this condition.

Diseases, including Amyotrophic Lateral Sclerosis (ALS, or Lou Gehrig's Disease), Parkinson's disease, Alzheimer's disease, Huntington's disease, and Dyslexia, to mention a few, all affect speech or the sound of the voice.

A person with cancer of the voice box sometimes must have it surgically removed, in which case, he or she may be able to speak using a mechanical larynx. The most common such device is called the electrolarynx, a battery powered, electrical apparatus that produces the vibrations necessary for speech. Not all these devices look the same and they are custom made to meet the specific needs of those who need them.

I used to frequent horse shows and I knew a man then with a voice that had an extremely high pitch, not within the normal voice range for an adult male. I have heard that when he was young, a horse kicked him in the throat. The injury permanently damaged his voice box.

Chapter Thirteen:
THE EAR

In order to hear the color tone voices, we're going to look at the ear that identifies the different colors. The structure of the ear can be divided into three sections: the outer ear, the middle ear, and the inner ear. The outer ear contains the pinna, which is, basically, a hole in the head, also referred to as the auricle. It captures and directs sounds and gives us its origin, like whether it is off to the right or left, high or low, before us or behind us. The eight different locations for the sound to travel are: up, down, left, right, forward, or back, upper right, lower left, and vice versa. The higher the sound in pitch, the more it is focused in the middle of the pinna; thus, middle is a yellow voice, which has a high pitch, is toward the middle. Remember, the highest sound is yellow, without hurting your ears, and a different color sound will take place in a different location of the pinna. Next is the auditory canal, which connects the outer ear to the middle ear. In the middle ear is the eardrum, also called the tympanic membrane. Behind the tympanic membrane, the ossicles consist of three bones: the hammer, anvil and stirrup.

In the middle ear the mechanical wave changes into vibrations. The stirrup uses fluid of the inner ear to create a compression wave within the fluid. Part of the middle ear includes the Eustachian tube, which connects to the mouth and equalizes pressure within the ear.

The inner ear consists of an oval window attached to a fluid filled structure called the cochlea, a snail-shaped organ lined with 20,000 or more hair-like nerve cells. It performs one of the most critical jobs to help us hear. It is in the cochlea that vibrations transmitted from the eardrum through the tiny bones are converted into electrical impulses, which are then sent along the auditory nerve to the brain. The cochlea connects to the basilar membrane, a stiff structural element that separates two liquid-filled tubes running along its coil to the auditory nerve.

You may have heard of something called human echolocation or facial vision. A change in air pressure occurs when you approach an obstacle or object. Persons with human echolocation abilities can sense the presence of such an object without being able to see it. Not everyone has this ability. I first noticed this when I was in high school, which is for me, a facial vision that needs to be at head level. The object before me becomes darker in sound when I am getting closer to it. Of course this is the location of the sound echoes bouncing back to me. The sound does not have the same quality as an open area. This perception varies from person to person in those who have the ability and also influences how well they hear.

Chapter Fourteen:
CAUSES OF HEARING LOSS

Some people hear better than others, regardless of whether the sounds are loud or soft. This is due to the value of the sound, in the color of the hue, and in the density of the object heard. What any person will pick up in a sound will be different from what others hear. Normal hearing frequency measured in hertz is about 20 to 20,000 Hz. The sound frequencies for a normal hearing person are about 15 to 18,000 waves, or cycles, per second. Thus, hearing frequency alone can make a voice sound different from person to person.

There are numerous reasons for hearing loss, including conditions such as tinnitus, osteitis, presbycusis and auditory fatigue. Tinnitus, or ringing in the ears, is only evident within the ringing sound and is not apparent in the higher frequencies.

Osteitis is caused by an inflammation of the bone structure of the ear. Presbycusis is caused by aging and mostly found in the higher frequencies. Auditory Fatigue has no set frequencies, high or low.

Hearing loss can result from an injury, such as when you listen to music at about 110 to 120 decibels. The decibel is the unit of loudness of a sound going through the ears. The safest decibel is 85, according to research. Note Sound Frequency refers to the number of waves of sound energy that pass a fixed point each second.

Some of the terms like "PP" mean "push pull." This, by the way, is a means of amplifying a sound to a higher intensity with less distortion. On the other hand, C-compression is a limiter for how loud a hearing aid will go.

The dispenser of a hearing aid can adjust the aid's maximum amount of sound that it will produce to the highest amount of sound that the hearing aid is capable of putting out. This means that a 90 decibel output adjustment will create 140 decibels of sound from the aid. Because ears come in different sizes, when you are fitted for a hearing aid, a mold of the ear is created. An ill-fitted aid may provide diminished sound.

Chapter Fifteen:
OTHER VOICES, WORDS, SAYINGS, AND CHANGING COLORS

Mankind has relied upon the sound of his fellow human beings' voices since the beginning of time. Some scholars believe Hebrew was the first known language. In the Holy Bible, in Genesis, Chapter 11, it is written that, originally, there was only one language. People in that era decided to build a tower reaching up to God, the tower of Babel; but the Lord thwarted their efforts by splitting their language into many different languages, which were then scattered throughout earth. Today, there are about 6000 known spoken languages. I have been told that English is the hardest language to learn, with Spanish you roll your tongue, and German is a throaty language. In Hebrew, hello, goodbye and peace is the same word - Shalom. You can tell which it is by the context or circumstances. Aloha in Hawaiian means hello, goodbye, I love you, and a few other things. Its meaning is determined by how it is said. In Russian, please and you're welcome are the same word - pozhalujsta.

In English, we have homonyms like sun and son. The sun is beating down hot and making your son sweat. Of course these words have different spellings. With idioms, the words are spelled the same but mean something slightly different. For example, the dog is barking, but you are barking up the wrong tree.

The first place that the word "voice" comes up in the Bible is in Genesis Chapter 3, verse 8. It says:

> *And they heard the voice of the LORD God walking in the garden in the cool of the day: and Adam and his wife hid themselves from the presence of the LORD God amongst the trees of the garden. (KJV)*

This refers to the story of Adam and Eve, when they both ate the apple from the tree of the knowledge of good and evil. Although in Genesis, Chapter 1, verse 3, it uses the word "said," which, of course, means the voice had to do it. It says "And God said Let there be light: and there was light" (KJV).

But what does God's voice sound like? The best answer, I found is in Ezekiel, Chapter 43, verse 2, where it says:

> *And, behold, the glory of the God of Israel came from the way of the east: and his voice was like a noise of many waters: and the earth shined with his glory. (KJV)*

The inner voice or the voice you hear in your head is your own. Some of us sometimes speak aloud when we think, or "think out loud." Just as long as you don't answer yourself (this is what someone once told me in college), it is a sign of intelligence.

When I was growing up, I met some identical twins that sounded exactly alike to me. After a while, I could tell them apart though. Twins spend a lot of time together, so they naturally pick up many of the same speech mannerisms and patterns. I believe that twins brought up separately would sound different to me than those raised together.

It has always fascinated me how a ventriloquist can make his or her voice seem to be somewhere else in the room and adopt a different voice for their puppet or mannequin. They engage in conversation with the puppet, as if it is another "person." Yet, when doing so, the color of the ventriloquist's regular voice never changes, even when he or she is speaking in the other voice.

In psychology, people afflicted with dissociative identity disorders sometimes speak in different voices, too, which represent different personalities. Schizophrenics hear voices in auditory hallucinations. Other people exhibit a selective mutism. They typically don't talk in any given situation or speak only to certain people. They often remain silent and speak aloud only at home. Persons afflicted with Tourette's Syndrome (TS) often exhibit vocal tics, such as clearing the throat, sniffing, and grunting, and nonsensical sounds like sudden outbursts of obscenities, which affects only about 15% of TS sufferers. Some of the conditions mentioned here are present at birth; others come on later in life.

Did you know that a person hypnotized will respond to the hypnotist's voice, as well as trust it? Hypnotism is actually a wakeful state with focused attention coupled by heightened suggestibility and diminished perceptual awareness. Scottish surgeon James Braid (c. 1841) called it "a peculiar condition of the nervous system, induced by a fixed and abstracted attention of the mental and visual eye, on one object, not of an exciting nature."

In Bio-linguistics, animals can pronounce not only words but whole phrases, but not the way we do. Animals' vocal sounds range from a variety of tones and octaves, which mean many things to them. They may respond to our commands, like "come here," or "shut up." Dogs and cats rely heavily on their sense of smell and may perceive smells humans cannot detect, perhaps even from hearing the commands we utter.

Dogs and cats have vocal cords, but of course they do not use them to talk. They have their own ways of communicating. Cats, for instance, are capable of making over 100 different vocal sounds. Dogs can only make 10. When a dog or cat growls, the sound comes through their vocal cords. A growl for a dog is emitted in different pitches but always softer than the growl of a cat. Barking, of course, is not softer than meowing.

Hissing by a cat, however, does not involve the vocal cords. When a cat purrs, this sound originates in the vocal cords.

In birds, the voice comes from the syrinx. Most birds make sounds, usually called singing, that are unintelligible to humans. Parrots can say about 500 words or more, including human sayings, singing, or phrases. Nevertheless, while singing these words, they usually bear no relation to the events going on around them.

The loudest animal on Earth is the blue whale. The deep vocalizations of a blue whale can build up to 180 decibels or more. Why? Some researchers think the sounds are navigation signals between groups of whales. Others believe it is merely communication beyond what humans can understand.

I love how some animals and sea creatures can change colors. Chameleons can camouflage themselves, blending into their surroundings. Some of the colors that they can change are red, yellow, orange, brown, to blue, light blue, green, turquoise, pink, purple, and black. Their chromatophores are special cells that lay in layers underneath their transparent outer skin, which allows them to change colors. Each layer takes part in the change, even with the pigment granules located in their cytoplasm.

On the other hand, cephalopods -octopuses, squid, and cuttlefish, can change color faster than a chameleon. They also can change their body shape and texture and can hide or "disappear" in a cloud of ink. The colors are believed to reflect the mood they are in. For an octopus, stark white means they are frightened, and they are fiery red when angry. The rest of the time, it is thought that they blend in with their surroundings.

Chapter Sixteen:
FACTS OF COLORS IN WHAT YOU SEE AND HEAR EVERY DAY

The voice takes a traveling route through a day. In the morning it is undeveloped, but by afternoon, it is up and running in what we all perceive to be a person's regular voice. By the end of the day, it is pretty well worn down, depending on how much a person has talked throughout the day. Its value and the density have reached the limits of their boundaries. With time alone and by influence the voice can change, but its shape does not change at all. If you are tired, or if you have just woken up in the morning, your words will come out slowly. Along with the value, your breathing is affected. A person that is physically out of shape often speaks faster, corresponding with his or her faster heart rate and breathing.

A slow voice reveals stress, such as a person suffering from a headache, or even one who is lying. You can hear the stress in the tone of the voice. If the news someone relays to you is good or bad, their tone will be, correspondingly, up or down. This is evident in the value alone. It does not change the hue or density of their voice.

There are two values, negative and positive, correlating with beliefs and the feelings one holds toward the person to whom he or she is speaking. You can often tell when someone is glad to see you or not, can't you? If you get along with a person, the density never changes, but the value can still be sad or angry. Remember the second part of the hue is the personality. This is always negative or positive the whole time, day in and day out. The voice changes within a week, too, and assumes the patterns of everyday life. To me, almost everybody sounds tired on Mondays, but on Fridays, they sound both tired and glad. But this shows in the value of the voice.

You and the friends that you hang out with interpret each others' voices. For example, if your friend finds a favorite CD he lost, when he tells you he found it, you will hear the excitement in his voice. If you know this friend well, you could perceive it so quickly you might even finish off his sentence for him when he tells you about it. A friend asked me once, if she could find someone that has the same color hair, and the same build, and height, would they have the same voice color, since they look very similar? No, one color tone does not match up with another. By this, one may have a blue voice, and the other will have some kind of green voice, but if both are blue, then you have the different shades, brightness, and so on. I have noticed in dating, the male usually goes for the voice colors that are opposite of his color, and vice versa, the females goes for the opposite as well. These opposite voices are better suited for each other. I noticed that if a male blue voice dates a female with a blue voice; watch out, they will clash!

When I was growing up, I heard catchy phrases and sayings. Anyone from my generation or older will know the name of the baseball announcer who said "holy cow" when a player got a home run? Yes, it was Harry Caray. One of the catchy phrases I used in high school was "that's what makes America great" and I remember others said "cool beans."

The traits that are implicit in an individual and that reveal thoughts and feelings are what I call a person's trademark. There is someone I know who always says to me, "love is in the air," referring to my last name, which is, of course, Love. Another person I know often calls me "good for nothing," but I know she is joking. These are obvious trademarks, set forth by these individuals' frequent use of the same words.

I have noticed subtle trademarks, too. For instance, most of the Lindas and Georges I have ever known sound very much alike to me. I believe that this is because I rely on my memories of the first Linda and George I ever met and then compare all the others to them. I have met quite a few people with these names; they are common names. But only a few do not immediately sound like a Linda or a George to me. They act like their names, but the Lindas and Georges do have different color tones. There are exceptions to every rule. Just like the sayings "redheads are hyper" and "blondes have more fun," there are always exceptions to the rule.

This has brought up a question for me though; I wonder what George Washington's voice sounded like. As I said before, not absolutely all Georges' voices sound alike. I wonder would our first president's voice be low and deep, or more in the mid-range?

I have read that George Washington was around 57 years of age when he became president of the United States. There were no cameras back then, but the pictures that are out there reveal that he had white hair. Powdered wigs were in style in those days, but Washington, it is said, actually put powder in his hair, to make it white. Perhaps this was a way of making him stand out in a crowd and look distinguished.

Something else that I have noticed is, if I incorrectly assume someone's name is different than it actually is, such as believing a person's name is Ken who turns out to be named something different, I tend to continue to regard this person as Ken. I think this is because he still sounds like a Ken. Similarly, a girl named Cathy might sound like a Dana to me. Whenever this happens, it is difficult to remember the person's real name when I hear his or her voice. Fortunately, this occurs rarely.

In a group, male and female voices usually produce the same color tone as a result of the influences of the individuals within the group. You inherit your voice. On both sides of my family the colors blue, red and yellow are present. I have noticed that when a married couple talks, their voices blend together into one color and it works well if their individual colors are opposite of each other, too. For example, a husband with a blue voice and a wife with a red voice may produce the color purple. This of course is in a conversation and the voices blend together. Yes, I can actually hear incompatibilities in colors within married couples' voices. A woman can be the color blue, which doesn't blend well with a man who has a blue voice. A blue voice blends well with a green voice. Because of these color perceptions, I can often tell whether a couple is truly meant to be together, but again, this is faulty. If there is a divorce involving a female with a red voice and a man with a blue voice, I believe they just did not match perfectly for some other reason.

Whenever a person talks to a baby, they use their upper voice. Males use their falsetto voice and women use their head voice. I have noticed this is true even when the people are strangers to the baby and its parents; if later they become friends, the upper voice is rarely used. When a child is around age 3, they stop speaking to it using their upper voices.

The upper voice is also used when talking to pets and plants (all our friends do not always have two feet). Liking animals and plants myself (the same is true of reptiles and insects), I use my upper voice as a way of saying "I love you" to them. The way you speak to others is a mirror of the way they you want them to react toward you.

Almost no one likes hearing himself or herself on tape. The color is fine, but the shade cast out by the tape player is different and unfamiliar. Other people on the tape sound like themselves to you, but not your own voice. Most people are very self-conscious about this until they become accustomed to the sound of their own voices.

Very few people talk in their sleep, but for those that do, it can occur in any stage of the sleep cycle. It involves the utterance of speech, or a word or two, every now and then, while sleeping. It is still the color of your own voice.

One summer, some friends and I engaged in a swimming pool game of guessing what each other were saying beneath the water. We would each go under to listen. A voice cannot travel through water, even if you shout. The volume will barely raise and a lot of bubbles will appear. Additionally, all voices sound alike under water.

My younger sister and I made tapes called "Different Sound Effects." We would usually go up to ten sounds and we had to then identify them, of course by sound. At the end of the tenth sound, my sister and I would go through and say what each sound was. I excelled at identifying each sound on the tape even when my sister made one without me present. One time, I tried twenty different sounds, but I could not remember them all.

Sometimes people deliberately change their voices to imitate other people's voices for entertainment or other reasons. One of the best voice impressions I have heard was on the Johnny Carson show when Johnny imitated Ronald Reagan. It sounded exactly like Reagan to me. It may interest you to know that, according to some sources, way back in the 1800s on the frontier, some Indians could imitate a white man's speech perfectly.

If you hear an announcer you do not know on an intercom or radio, questions comes to your mind: what does this person look like? Do I like him or her? By the voice alone, you decide if you like the announcer. You form an opinion. If later, you meet this person, they will likely look completely different than you imagined from the voice you heard. You might see the announcer's picture in a magazine, or have an encounter at some fundraiser. After seeing this person, his or her voice will sound different to you because it is no longer being heard on the radio or intercom.

Now, bring your mind back to the question, do I like this announcer? While you may find appearance off-putting, you could still decide you enjoy listening to his or her voice on the radio. You have had to get to know that announcer all over again because you saw the whole person.

Age is hard to determine in the voice, except in children and the elderly. When a voice advances in years, the hue starts to fade, some faster than others. An elderly person's voice eventually becomes shaky. I can usually recognize old age in a person around the age of 80. Children, on the other hand, I can recognize from age 3 to about age 11. Remember, the voice is still being developed at this age. From age 18 to around 50, I have the most difficulty determining peoples' ages.

Because accents are prevalent throughout the world, people in countries that speak the same language may sound different. When people live together, they come to speak similarly, enunciating certain words, using regional slang, etc. Actors often learn other accents to play a role. For example, if an American southwest native is an actor who must play a character from England, he or she may imitate "the queen's English," rather than speaking Cockney, or another variation of an English accent; and certainly they will not speak their parts in their normal American southwest accent.

Chapter Seventeen:
THE COLORS OF LIFE EXPERIENCES

Around 1996, a rerun of the old television show, *Mork and Mindy* was on, which I hadn't heard for about 17 years, which was before I lost my eyesight. The voice of Mork instantly conjured up the actor Robin Williams to me. The next day I mentioned this to someone and was told the character, Mork, was played by Robin Williams. I had not been aware of that back when I had my sight. Since losing my eyesight, I have watched two or three movies with Williams in it. Now I have a face to put his voice, which is Mork from Ork's face. Williams' voice is red all the way through. It's very deep red when it first starts off, and changes to a lighter shade of red in the center of the voice. Of course this sound bounces back and forth between the value and the hue, even when he is not acting.

I also saw the movie, *Grease,* back when I still had my eyesight. I was absolutely crazy about Olivia Newton-John. I can still clearly remember the way she looked. Not long ago, I met her after one of her concerts here in St. Louis, Missouri. It had been 25 years since I saw *Grease.* I know a lot has happened to Olivia since she starred in the movie and that she is much older now, but just seeing her live, in living color, and talking to her, I felt she was still very beautiful today—and I was told that is true. Olivia's voice is blue-silver. The outside value is a beautiful blue, and the center hue is shiny silver.

When I was in high school, someone once asked me to describe what Casey Kasem looks like. Kasem hosted the American Top 40 pop music hits every Sunday from 1970 until 1988. I enjoyed hearing him talk about each song he played. I told my high school friend "he is 6 feet tall, a tall proud American with his shoulders back, with a moustache and a brown beard, brown hair, and wire-framed glasses." The reply I got, I could not believe. She said "he is not tall or standing straight, but a short stocky man, cleanly shaven, who wears black shoe polish in his hair." (Incidentally, I have not read anywhere that he ever wore shoe polish in his hair.) The difference in how I saw Kasem and how he was described to me came as a shock. His voice has a red-blue to it. Of course the dark red will be the hue in the center of the voice. I have noticed that when he sighs, the lighter blue in the value is present because of the sound going out slower. For example, when you hear him say "and now" you hear a sigh with the word now.

This reminds me of another day back in high school when, in one of my classes, the teacher talked about going to New York for some kind of meeting where she ordered her breakfast in the hotel restaurant. She said she was seated beside a businessman who began telling her about himself, what he did for a living. She told him about her job, too. On the other side of the businessman sat a black man drinking coffee. The businessman turned toward him and asked, "What do you do for a living?" The black man told him he was Martin Luther King's father and that he had been with him on the day he was shot and killed. Until I heard that story, I had thought Martin Luther King was a white man. It makes me now respect the man more for what he has done. I am sure that I saw some pictures of Martin Luther King but perhaps forgot them, or lost that memory as a result of my brain injury. The value of King's voice is deep gray. The hue in the center is medium red. When he gave speeches, the voice was fuller because the words were slower and louder, making it a full sound, the hue has much more sound in it. Unlike Casey Kasem, you can hear the value of the sound in the sigh. With King, you hear a gray sound more because his voice is going out slower than going in.

On another occasion, a group of Spanish students visiting the U.S. came to our school and somehow ended up in my Communications class where no one could speak Spanish. We communicated with the Spanish students by drawing pictures. I noticed at this time that it does not matter if a person speaks English or not, his or her voice has the same color tones as English-speaking people.

This brings up the question, what do you think of when you hear the names Stephen King and Vincent Price? What does your mind automatically think of? Spooky and scary, since one writes scary books and the other is in scary movies. King has a medium gray voice and Price has a mint green voice. I love reading and watching these kind of stories. I also love to listen to the old time radio mysteries, where you imagine in your mind what is going on. In a silent movie, I hear only music because there is no talking. Sometimes, I cannot tell if the movie is in color or in black and white, but sometimes I can tell they are not in color from the music.

I have noticed about 80 percent of the commercials have music in them to fit the commercial.

Once my parents got new carpeting and new furniture for the family room, but for two days the room was completely empty. I loved the echo affect, which made voices sounded fuller and louder. Carpet dampens sound, especially in a classroom. The more open space there is in a room, the more it echoes.

When I was young, I remember visiting caves and being fascinated by the echoes I heard inside them, even when talking in my regular voice. When I shouted, I could hear the echo's delay and repeat, two or three times, depending on how long the cave was. Your voice still sounds like your voice no matter how big the echo; just the texture of the sound is different. Like for example, when you step into an elevator and the door closes, the sound changes from an open sound to a closed sound.

There are ways you can make sound fuller or lighter, affecting its tone color. You can make it dull or bright. You can also change the width and depth of a sound. You can change the rate and duration. There are different textures within sound, too, and sounds have their own shape in their own tone color. One of my favorite sounds on my reverb machine when I record music is the flanger. I love how heavy or light you can make that sound. You can control the feedback and the shape, and expand the sound. When I record vocals, I love the sounds of the wet plate and the chorus. Consider your own family room—you know the shape of it—so that is its shape to you in your mind; there is also, similarly, shapes in sounds and voices. Of course, a family room you can change, but the voice you cannot.

A man once asked me the color of his voice. I said, "the hue is blackish-gray, and the value is blue." He then told me those were the colors he was wearing that day. When a girl asked me the color of her voice, I said blue. She told me that was also the color of her eyes. The question is did they try to find something similar to what they are familiar with in their lives? I believe so. This is how we all make sense of the world, by relating what is new to us to what is familiar.

We all got to know at an early age that green is go at the traffic light, red is stop, and yellow means slow down. Regarding sounds relating to colors, with red, I see a police or ambulance siren, a sign of danger, get out of the way. A sunburn on your face is red and it is a different shade of red when your face gets very cold, usually when winter temperatures drop. When you hear a tornado warning on the radio or television, or outside, you get ready for a possible tornado. This sound is interesting because it has a red-yellow two-part sound. The red part is the lower part of the sound, and yellow is the upper part. Why do I think this? Because it's telling me to be aware of possible danger, like the traffic light. A fire in the fireplace has an interesting sound. Because of the flames on the logs, the sound of burning goes in and out. The colors fascinated me. What I remember is red, orange, blue, green, and yellow intertwining together. So the sound that I hear in front of the fireplace is red, orange, blue, green, and yellow. When you hear a news paper rattling, what do you see, a black and white newspaper? Yes, just like when you are in the other room and you hear someone put the coffeepot back on the burner, you can see the pot, and the coffee inside.

Like sighted people, I cannot imagine what it is like for a person to be born blind. They have not acquired a memory of colors, so they can have no concept of them. From talking to a native blind person, I learned that he regards red as hot and blue as cold. Interestingly, when I touch or taste something cold, it is the color blue, and if something is hot, it is red to me. For taste, since I cannot taste, I can relate this to what a native blind person is talking about. When I hear the word happy, I think of red, too; but for sad, the color is blue. I regard the word or idea of "mediocre" as purple, which is, of course, a blend of red and blue, happy and sad. This, too, goes with my mind, colors of moods. (See "A List of Letters and Music Notes in Colors").

There is a negative and positive side to each color. In my grade school, a pink slip, which was really just a wrinkled piece of colored paper, meant that you were bad. A gold slip, however, was given to you if you were good. A color is a color to me even though I never actually saw those slips. I always wished for mine to be red or silver because those are my favorite colors.

I once became fascinated with mood rings, which were popular in the late 70s and early 80s. There is also a negative and positive side to each color. On the color chart that came with those rings some of the different shades of bluish-green meant "Somewhat Relaxed" or "Upbeat." Some of the different shades of dark blue meant "Liveliness", or "Moonstruck." White, which the ring never turned on me, meant "frustrated." I cannot understand that one. My mood ring always turned red. One of the things red signified was "you are going over the edge"; other meanings for red were "you are angered" and "sarcasm."st

However, the following colors have only meaning, and not much positive or negative. I went to South Carolina with Student Venture, a Christian-based youth group from my old high school. On the way home on the bus, we stopped somewhere in Tennessee at a bus station. Someone there showed one of my fellow students something they described as the four spiritual laws, but there were no words, just colors in it. What they said was, "the color white is heaven, black is sin, and red represents Christ's blood." Some believe in the theory that the color black, in the dream world, is a sign of death. In Christianity, death can be both physical and spiritual.

Each holiday has its own color; the color green is of course St. Patrick's Day, and red, white, and blue is the Fourth of July. Green and red is Christmas, and red and white is Valentine's Day. Even the colors of roses for Valentine's Day have meaning. Red is the most common. A very deep red is for lovers. A bright red rose is for passion, and cardinal red is desire. An open red rose means I am still in love with you. A yellow one means friendship or happiness in your home and also means I am sorry. The white roses mean innocence and loyalty. They also stand for purity and sincerity and are used in weddings. Black of course is death and sorrow, used for funerals. The color peach shows of appreciation, and thanks.

There was a battery tabletop brain challenge game called Simon that was popular in the 70s. Blue, in this game, sounded blue to me and it was the lowest note on Simon Says. It also appeared to me to have a square shape. The color red came next. Red sounded red to me. The shape also sounded like a circle. Green sounded to me like it should be the color yellow and a triangle. Finally, the color yellow sounded forlorn to me. It sounded like a sand color in an octagon shape. The color blue, the lowest note on Simon Says is the low A, yellow is C sharp, red is E, and green is high A. Interestingly, on the piano, these same four colors spell out the A chord. The notes on the piano get a different color because of the way they sound. Because of their brightness, their shades vary.

One sound never changes. It is the hum of the refrigerator. It is tuned to B flat. For this sound I picture pale blue because it keeps food cold and fresh. Most, if not all, electric motors run on 60 cycles per second.

The sound of a lawn mower is tuned to B flat also, but the sound is green because the lawn mower is cutting the green grass. Although most car horns are tune to B flat, I see red, a sign of danger, or get out of my way, because I have somewhere to go. Airplane turbines are also tuned to B flat, but I picture a blue-gray sound, because looking out the window, you see the sky and clouds. On my third album the song titled "I Am So Tired Of Hearing B Flat," I go through a lot of things that are tuned to B flat.

The train whistle also fascinates me, and a fog horn or the departure signal bell on a big cruise ship. The fog horn has a two interval sound, but like the doorbell, the second interval is darker than the first one. The doorbell is red, but the fog horn and the train whistle have a multi-colored sounds, colors of their own built in layers. The cruise ship has a darker sound than the train whistle, but the colors are the same. I remember a color wheel chart back in first grade in the corner of the classroom. This perfectly fits the color tones of the train whistle.

Complementary colors are the opposite colors across from each other on the color wheel chart. The lowest color tone that I hear in the train whistle is red. The opposite, next to the lowest red tone, is green. Next, the third level is blue. The fourth level then is orange. The fifth is purple. The top-level color is yellow. In the train whistle, the lowest color tone to the highest is red, green, blue, orange, purple, and yellow.

There are other day sounds I observe, such as grasshoppers and locusts from the start of spring to about mid-fall. Their colors are green and white. When the sound gets louder, it is green; when the sound is softer, it is white. This is because I remember that trees and leaves are green, and remember, the basis of all sound is white.

These sounds are not blended unless there are two or more groups of what I believe are grasshoppers or locusts making this sound. This gives each green more green, because the white does not cancel it out to any extent. But if there is just one group of grasshoppers or locusts, I see the green going up as the white dies out.

I am especially fascinated with the cicada sounds that come only every thirteen years. To me, they emit a red sound, a very loud red sound.

When I had my eyesight, I caught lightning bugs, or fireflies. I loved the way they lit up in my hands. I even had one in a jar, for a little bit.

Now I love listening to the night sounds. It seems they communicate with each other. I have noticed sounds coming from the left in late July and August that make only two or three clicks, like a car trying to start up. Then off to the right, I will hear the clicks answering back. Then a different group will respond farther away. I love listening to the frogs and crickets as well as the other unknown night sounds. They have excellent rhythm and stay together in one beat.

The following comes from my writing in high school, which brought me to the idea that voices have also have colors:

> *Flowing connecting colors in a pie shape form. Such colors as blue, green, yellow and red fit together into one. It makes different shades of brightness and dullness, but other sorts of colors are present too. However, only one can be seen in a place of time or can change to another color in few seconds. Take it the way you like it, but this is only your imagination.*

Chapter Eighteen:
VOICES IN DREAMS

In my dreams, colors are in accord with voices that I remember and identify with by their voiceprint. The voices in dreams have fascinated me for a long time for both their "off the wall" and familiar places.

There is something very strange when a person that you never knew appears in a dream. Their actions do not match. Nine out of ten times it takes place somewhere different. Then you have a normal dream where nothing worth note happens. In my dreams, there must be an action of some sort before I know the dreams colors. The sounds always come first and the pictures follow. The sounds and voices and situation can be nice and happy, but I also know nightmares.

I know that I dream in color because I can remember the colors from when I once could see them. I have been told that if you dream in color, you are creative. Apparently non-creative types dream in black and white.

Since I dream in color, however, I'm describing these colors only because they occur in four dreams I will describe here shortly.

The color red is an invitation to raw energy, and has to do with force and vigor. Red also is an intense passion, and has to do with aggression, power, and courage. It also has to do with impulsiveness and passion. On the more negative side, the color red invites a lack of energy. This has to do with the feeling of being tired or lethargic. Like I said before, red is danger, like the stop light. It also has to do with violence, blood, shame, and the feeling of rejection. Lastly it has to do with the feeling of sexual impulses and urges, an indication that you should "think about your actions."

The color gold has to do with reflections of spiritual reward. It also has to do with richness and refinement, and the enhancement of your surroundings. Also gold is a sign of your determination and unyielding nature. Green then is a sign of a positive change. It also means good health, growth, and fertility. It stands for healing, and the word hope, and for the word vigor. It also stands for vitality, peace, and serenity. The color green is the color of go-straight-ahead. On the negative side, green is the lack of experience in some assignments. It also means you are conscious of your environment. You have drive to work and gain recognition and to say that you're independent. Finally, in the color green, you think of money, wealth, and jealousy.

Gray means the dream is surrounded in fear, and in depression. You are frightened, in poor health, confused or ambivalent. You probably feel emotionally detached, or distant from things or others. The color white is a sign of purity, and the word perfection. It also means peace, innocence, cleanliness, awareness of what is going on, and new beginnings. On the flip side, the color white is a clean slate or a cover up. Brown of course stands for the earth, the ground or grounded. It also is practicality, domesticity, and physical comfort. It might be conservatism, and a materialistic character trait. The color black is a sign of the unknown. It also shows unconscious feeling, and danger, and is very mysterious. Black means darkness, and of course death. Black is also mourning, and feeling rejected. Black can mean hate or malice, not feeling loved, or having the support that you need. On the positive side, this color also indicates a better understanding of you, your potential and possibilities. Finally this implies the hidden spirituality and the divine qualities of you.

Voices in a dream are like voices heard when awake. You can tell whether a person likes you or not from the sound. In your waking life, you may wish that a particular person treated you better or you wanted to get to know someone more. If the object of your attention will not give you the time of day, the disappointment resonates in your unconscious mind. This kind of dream I call the "voice action dream." The person does not sound like your friend, but acts like a friend. This is demonstrated in the following dream.

A girl I really liked ignored me in real life. In my dream, she and I were in a movie theater. The seats were red velvet and the aisle was a red carpeted ramp going down with gold rims on each side, the silver screen in front. It looked like a normal movie theater, and there was nothing unusual about it, or what I remember about it, back in the 1970's. I was seated in the aisle seat and she was down the row against the wall. She wore a mask so I would not recognize her, but of course I knew it was her. The voice was saying in the mask, you do not know me, but you would, if I did not have this on.

Nine times out of ten, you will not succeed in getting around the mask. But someone who knows you very well will still know you despite any masks. In a dream, it's normal to hear things or objects talk, but obviously not in real life. There is something in the mind that tells you who people are, if just by their presence, or perhaps when you hear them laugh. They cannot change their footsteps, or the way their body looks and acts.

In my dream, the movie was getting ready to start, and the girl with her mask on got up and walked past me to leave. I never knew if she realized that I knew who she was. But she was recognizable probably because of her body, mannerisms, and so on. (On the other hand, it is hard for me to know what a person truly looks like based only on descriptions from others.) The mask then was the voice action, the key element in the dream, because the situation revolved around the mask.

My friend's mask was gold, red, and black. It had a gold metal face plate. It had two holes for the eyes, and two holes on the raised nose, and an opening for the mouth. The holes were outline in red. The cloth back of the mask, wrapped around her head and holding the mask in place, was black.

The mask's gold was a sign of her determination, a fear that I would recognize her and enhance her surroundings. Red was a sign of danger. If I said anything to her, or she to me, it would reveal that I knew her. The color black was the unknown, which is what she wanted, therefore she wore a mask.

Colors have their own voice in dreams and the following "off-the-wall" dream exemplifies this. This is called a voice color dream. I was at Notre-Dame's bell tower, and I was standing at the edge looking at the sunset. How awesome it looked! Red, orange, yellow, blue, and even the pink and purple blending together. The colors had voices blending in together too, but I could not read or understand the beautiful words, nor could I make any sense of it all. But they had friendly beautiful voices for each color, and I was seeing and believing them in my eyesight. The wind was not blowing, the bells were not ringing. I took a step out over the edge, and instead of falling, I started mixing into the colors of the sunset as I drifted farther and farther away from the edge. I was disappearing into the colors, but I was not scared. Of course this was just a dream. Obviously, you cannot do this in real life. The colors here had their own voices, and I knew it was okay to step out over the edge. The key element in this dream was the sunset.

When you dream about a sunset, it means you're at the end of one cycle. It was time for rest, and a time to think things over. This was interesting to me because I was at a point of my life when I was starting to do things totally alone, like doing laundry and fixing my own meals.

The colors in the dream had their own voices. Because the voices were calm and pleasing to my mind, they indicated peace. This exemplifies the definition of hearing voices in your dream. Pale colors suggest weakness while dark colors imply passion and intensity. Bright colors mean your awareness of what you are doing. By this definition, I was feeling mixed up, a mixture of colors, and I had to take a step into a larger world where I did not know if I could sink or swim.

Now I am going to examine one of my nightmares. This took place right beside my front porch. Here goes. I was by the front porch, and I was standing between the gray concrete sidewalk and the green bushes. I was ten years old at the time. Off to my left was a wooden black post holding the front porch covering. I could see the red brick wall, the front porch windows, and the front door. The moon had just gone down, and the sky was gray, getting ready for the sun to come up. The only things I could hear was the wind blowing the leaves on the trees, and the sound of traffic from a nearby perpetually busy highway. At my feet were sand dollars and the sand dollars went all the way around the green bushes. I thought it was neat. The sizes ranged from a silver dollar size to a small dinner plate size. I was so busy picking up the sand dollars and looking at them, that a green snake, with its red glowing beady eyes came out of a man size hole, wrapped around both of my ankles, and pulled me into the hole. When the hole got above my head, I woke up.

The key element of this dream was the sand dollars. If not for them, I would of not have been at there. The sand dollars did not have a voice saying "pick me up." I picked them up because of my fascination with them (unlike the voice action dream about the mask or the "voice color dream" about the sunset). The color brown for the sand dollars stands for the earth, because I was outside, beside a bush, and was looking at the sand dollars on the ground. The color gray then was the color of the sky; the moon had just gone down. Gray means I was surrounded in fear about the time, because I was only ten years old. The snake and the bushes were green because in the back of my mind I was conscious or keenly aware of my environment. The glowing red eyes stood for violence because the snake violently and quickly dragged me down in to the hole.

Now, finally, a normal dream. This dream was comfortable, I felt at home, and the voices in the dream talked were not scary. I was in a different country and recognized a girl there right away. Her mother was with her. I knew this from the voices of both of them. Her mother had the same color voice as her daughter, but she was a lot older. We were in their home. The house had a stairway going up to a living room off to the right. Straight ahead about two feet away was a white wall, and I could hear a stereo playing a song by Nirvana. Why, I do not know, because I am not a fan of that band and neither is my friend, the girl in the dream. The name of the song was "Smells Like Teen Spirit." I know that she had heard this song because after the basketball game, the college band and I would play it. Of course this was not one of the songs we had to learn for band to play at the basketball game. She and I did like listening to the music, but not the lyrics. The kitchen was off to the left of the stairway. The kitchen was in white. My friend and her mother were talking to me in the living room. My friend and her mother had hair that was shiny black and it stood out in the room. Both their voices were very light blue, and in the middle was medium silver, like in real life, and they were having a nice pleasant conversation, but what was being said was unclear to me, it could of been in their own language. I understood when they asked me a question, but what was said I don't remember. The color of the carpet was green, and so was the stairway. There was a table with a white vase holding red roses, and there was a black leather couch beside it. Everything in the room was beautiful to me, and I felt at home.

This friend's actual house looks nothing like it did in my dream. She and her mother both live in a very small apartment. In the dream, their house was quite large. This dream was normal; nothing was off-the-wall or different, just like normal everyday awake life. I felt at home like it would be in real life. The room was the key element of the dream because the situation took place in it, but the music was softly heard in the background and had no affect on the situation. (This was not a voice action dream about a mask or a voice color dream about the colors in the sunset.) A lot of things were white, the kitchen, the walls, and the vase, representing the purity, and innocence in the situation, since there was no anger, or yelling. It was a pleasant conversation with the mother, my friend, and me. The green carpet means peace, and the word hope, since my friend and I get along very well, and she gives me hope when I need it. For red, the roses mean intense passion, probably about how my friend and I feel about each other, because she is very important to me. Finally, the color black, the couch, and the color of my friend's and her mother's hair. These are the divine qualities in me and her since we are friends and understand each other well, and for me, getting along with her mother.

Chapter Nineteen:
DIFFERENT KINDS OF THERAPIES

Color has been around since mankind. There is a thing called Color Therapy, also called Chromo Therapy. It dates back to the ancient Egyptians. They thought colors were made up of sunlight, each designed to show a different appearance of the supreme good and influenced by the different characteristics of life. The colors you wear, which are often your favorite colors, have an effect on your emotional state. To me, it is the personality of a person that shows in one of these colors. Color therapy is a therapeutic tool, like visualization. It uses verbal suggestion to bring balance to energy in the places of our bodies that are lacking their state of being. It draws on the physical, emotional, spiritual, or mental things of life.

To be balanced, you need all the energy colors, and each color is unique. Red says you need safety in your life, and you should use your energy and passion wisely. Orange says that you need to have more fun in your life, and you should use your creativity to celebrate who you are, here and now. With yellow, you need to be more focused, directing your mind to positive and happy thinking, trusting your power and wisdom. Green indicates that you need to love yourself, allow yourself freedom; you need to forgive and to release stress. With blue, you need to trust yourself, and your intuition, you need to trust the universe, and to express yourself in a calm way. Indigo shows that you need to be true to yourself, to remember your true visions and dreams, and to find peace. Violet indicates that you need to use your personal power, and to allow spiritual evolution, you need to follow your inspiration and know yourself. You need all seven of these colors. If even one color is missing, something will be unbalanced in your life, things will go wrong. Each color is called a chakra. All the colors need to run smoothly to be balanced, just as a grandfather clock must have everything working right to keep the right time.

Color therapy also has to do with the Pineal glands, also known as the third eye that connects to the brain's control center, influence the daily rhythms of your life, like how you walk and talk. Colors are healing properties. They reveal how you feel. When a baby is born, lighter colors, such as pinks and blues, are usually chosen for the nursery. Their use will affect the mood in the baby's room.

When I grew up, my own bedroom was blue. My voice sounds blue-black. Someone who I related to had a yellow room and she has a yellow voice. Also, another person I related to had a pink room, but her voice is the color red, which is, of course, very close to pink. You inherit the color of your voice, but it can be influenced by other things. It can change, but its true essential color will remain.

I never forget looking at the different colored crayons in a crayon box. I did not have a favorite color back then, but there was a multicolored crayon that I loved. Different studies show that emotional reactions are caused by colors, which are unique to every individual. The things we are fascinated with, the things we like, their specific colors signal the brain and reveal areas where we are imbalanced. From your favorite to the least of your favorite colors, they will impact your life.

Different colors give off different wavelength frequencies, which can be positive or negative. These different frequencies bring about different effects on our physical and psychological functions. Most hospital hdallways are painted green because green is a calming color that reminds of us of open space, such as we see outdoors with the trees and grass. Many doctors' offices are also painted this color. Think, what if they were painted gray? Some might regard that color as peaceful while others consider it depressing.

The color yellow is one of the softer colors and is very pleasing to most people. If a room is painted red, some think of danger and feel anxious, like you do when a traffic light changes to red when you are driving through an intersection. Others may think of the word "love" when they see the color red, usually because of hearts and Valentine's Day.

Similarly, sound therapy helps physical and mental conditions through sound wave vibrations. If your health and emotional states are affected in any way, it is thought that your resonant frequencies are out of balance in your body. Treatment for this involves transmitting favorable sound to the affected area. Some of the healing sounds are voices and musical instruments. This is like listening to Pink Floyd or Beethoven, or whatever your music tastes. Other favorable sounds include nature, birds whistling in a jungle. Walking is also a stress reliever.

For example, if you have a bad day, you might pick up the phone and call your girlfriend just to hear her voice. You are relying on one of your favorite sounds to soothe you. Feeling a favorite sound's vibration and colors puts the mind at ease.

Finally this brings up music therapy. To me, the definition of music therapy involves the psychological, physiological, cognitive, communicative, and social function of the person. It elevates the mood, stimulates self-awareness, promotes social interaction, and helps the growth and development, and brings desired goals and outcomes. One of the things you can do with music therapy is to begin with melodic intonation therapy, which is when the singing voice is taken slowly to a chant and then to a regular talking voice. Melodic intonation therapy may be used after a brain injury, for example, to teach someone to talk again. Studies have shown that singing and talking take place in the brain in two different locations. So when you hear someone rapping or chanting, if falls between singing and talking. The rhythm almost fits together but is still separate. In one of my music therapy practicums, I also used lyric analysis, in which one looks at the words of a song and relates them to his or her life.

One of the songs that I have had a lot of luck with is "Bridge Over Troubled Water" by Simon and Garfunkel. I have used a few other songs in my work and sometimes my clients did not like the piece, but most of them love the words to "Bridge over Troubled Water."

Another thing you can do with music therapy, which I also learned in one of my practicums, is progressive and autogenic relaxation. In this, the music therapist voice tells you how to relax. In progressive relaxation, you tense the muscle groups of the body and in autogenic relaxation, you think of your muscle groups as being hot and heavy. An example of progressive relaxation: you tense your feet for five seconds and release. An example of autogenic relaxation: "your feet are hot and heavy".

Another thing in music therapy is the Guided Imagery of Music. In this, you listen to relaxation music as the music therapist's voice is guiding you to places like the beach or a forest of some kind. There are so many ways to go with music therapy, techniques for pain management to memory recall list just a few, and different populations to work with.

Lastly, I will talk about anger management, which I studied in one of my music therapy classes. tYou can do this on the piano or a drum. The client, or patient, acts out their anger on the instrument and then you can guide them to a more positive result. This is what you call the "iso principle". By this, you start with music that matches the person's feelings, mood, and their concerns, and gradually taking it to a more positive result by changing the style of music to have a more desired outcome.

Chapter Twenty:
VOICE TECHNOLOGIES

Some places are making machine gadgets with an activated voice. I think this is really neat. First, there is the voice changer. Today a few companies make voice changers, which can alter a voice to make it unrecognizable, like making a male sound like a female. It can even change the color tone of your own voice. If you wanted to sound like someone with an orange voice, you could. There is a variety of these machines available, which also range in price. Some companies will have the voice quality and the range set to your specifications, and some even include monster or alien voice options.

This brings up the vocoder. A vocoded analysis synthesis system is used for speech. The input goes through a multiband filter; and, from this, each band goes through an envelope follower, which then leads to the decoder. From there, the decoder takes the amplitude and applies it to the control signals to corresponding filters in a resynthesizer. The resynthesizer is a sound or voice played back to you of what you recorded in the decoder.

I have seen at music stores a device called a talk box, which modifies the sound of a musical instrument to make it sound human. By lip syncing or changing the shape of your mouth, you can control the modification of the talk box and make it "speak" or "sing."

An electronic voice phenomenon, or EVP, generates sounds that resemble a talking voice, but not a living human's voice, but rather, the voice of something preternatural. Some say that these sounds are static, stray radio transmissions and background noises, while others believe they could be of paranormal origin. Another theory about them is that the sounds could be a result of increasing the gain of the background sounds. In any event, they show up in the recordings that the equipment picks up.

Those who believe in this often claim a word or a phrase can be heard in these recordings. The number one choice for EVP is the use of portable digital voice recorders. In listening to what the recorders pick up, some claim it is like learning a new language. In paranormal explanations, it is theorized that these sounds could be a living human's imprinted thoughts arising out of an electronic medium by virtue of psychokinesis, which is movement of one or more objects using psychic energy. Some believe the sounds come from spirits or extraterrestrials; and finally, there are people who believe EVP is actually nature energies from other beings that are not of our dimension.

Another device useful for talking into a computer is called VRI, or voice recognition interface. VRI recognizes the voice pattern and sound quality of your voice. It probably would work with my best friend's voice too, as he sounds a lot like me. The VRI does not pick up the colors of voices the, but it does pick up the frequency. This reminds me of a time when my old best friend would say a name into his cell phone and it would dial the correct number. If I said the name, it would work for me too because my voice has almost the same frequency.

Years ago on the television show, *Star Trek*, a person could talk to a computer and the computer did what it was told. Today, we are actually there technologically. The visually impaired, like me, now enjoy the advantages of talking screen readers, scanning software, scales, calculators, watches, and dictionaries. I just wish their voices had more personality.

The last thing that I want to mention is the GPS, or global positioning system, a device that calculates the distance to a location. It is mainly designed for driving and walking and receives its information from satellite signals.

CONCLUSION

Picture a regular size box in your mind. You can see (in your mind) that the box is brown. In my mind I see these things day in and day out. When I am at the grocery store and I hear someone toss a box in their cart, I see a box (probably not brown) tossed into a silver metal cart. When hearing the glass freezer open, I see the silver trim and a jug of white milk. Where you check out, I can see someone reach to a silver rack and pick up original Dentyne gum, the cover red and white and the wrapper silver. When I walk in my front yard, I see the green grass below, the blue sky above, and the white puffy clouds in the sky. When someone tells me the stars are beautiful at night, I see a black night sky with the white stars and the yellow moon. When I am at a restaurant, you and I can hear kitchen noises, silverware being washed. I can see the silver sink (or a different color), and the silver colored silverware being washed. I relate to what I remember when I had my eyesight. My favorite sighted experience was the ocean when I was five years old in Florida. How beautiful the blue ocean was and still is with the waves coming in. I am standing on the beach enjoying the ocean breeze. Memories never die.

Everyone, whether he or she realizes it or not, gives the voices they hear their own distinctive color. My voice has been described by someone who recognizes this ability as blue-black. Another person said it was stone-washed gray. It really depends on the mind of the individual that perceives you. Even the colors you wear reveal your inner self. Your color preferences speak loudly without words and reflect your personality. We can change the texture of our hands by applying lotion, but not our fingerprints. The color of your voice is like a fingerprint; it is unique. There are no right or wrong answers. The color of your voice is what it is. Whether you like it or not, it is you. It has been told, like the old saying goes, the eyes are the windows to the Soul. To me the ears are the Doorways to the heart, as the voice is the foundation to your true self.

* * *

HELPFUL REFERENCES

Note: Biblical quotations and references mentioned in this book refer to the King James Version of the Holy Bible.

INTRODUCTION

THE HIDDEN SENSE: SYNESTHESIA IN ART AND SCIENCE (LEONARDO BOOK SERIES): CRETIEN VAN

VAN CAMPEN: 9780262514071: AMAZON.COM: BOOKS. N.P., N.D. WEB.

A LIFE OF SIR FRANCIS GALTON: FROM AFRICAN EXPLORATION TO THE BIRTH OF EUGENICS: NICHOLAS WRIGHT GILLHAM: 9780195143652: AMAZON.COM: BOOKS. N.P., N.D. WEB.

"CHARLES BONNET SYNDROME." INTERVIEW. ALL THINGS CONSIDERED. NPR NATIONAL PUBLIC RADIO, 30 JAN. 2008. RADIO.

CHAPTER ONE: DEFINING COLORS

THE COLORS IN A RAINBOW:

CHRISTIANSON, GALE E. ISAAC NEWTON. OXFORD: OXFORD UP, 2005. PRINT.

WAVELENGTHS OF LIGHT:

WAVELENGTH FREQUENCY/INTERVAL:

SERWAY, RAYMOND A., AND JERRY S. FAUGHN. HOLT PHYSICS. ORLANDO: HOLT, RINEHART AND WINSTON, 2009. PRINT.

LAMPS:

HTTP://INVENTORS.ABOUT.COM/OD/LSTARTINVENTIONS/A/LIGHTI NG_2.HTM

THE PHOTON CONCEPT:

THE ATOM:

ELECTRONS:

ELECTROMAGNETIC SPECTRUM:

HOUSE, J. E. INORGANIC CHEMISTRY. AMSTERDAM: ACADEMIC/ELSERVIER, 2008. PRINT.

COLOR CONSTANCY; ESTIMATED NUMBER OF COLORS:

GONYEA, MARK. A BOOK ABOUT COLOR. NEW YORK: HENRY HOLT AND, 2010. PRINT.

EWALD HERING:

HERING, EWALD. THEORY OF BINOCULAR VISION: EWALD HERING . [S.L.]: SPRINGER, 2012. PRINT.

NUMBER OF COLORS IN EXISTENCE:

HTTP://WWW.W3SCHOOLS.COM/HTML/HTML_COLORS.ASP

CHAPTER TWO: THE EYE

PARTS OF THE HUMAN EYE:

PHOTORECEPTORS:

OYSTER, CLYDE W. THE HUMAN EYE: STRUCTURE AND FUNCTION. SUNDERLAND, MA: SINAUER ASSOCIATES, 2006. PRINT.

COLOR BLINDNESS:

"ALL ABOUT COLOR BLINDNESS: A GUIDE TO COLOR VISION DEFICIENCY FOR KIDS (AND GROWN-UPS TOO)." : KAREN RAE LEVINE, FRANK WALLS, DR. TERRACE WAGGONER, T. J. WAGGONER: 9781477638880: AMAZON.COM: BOOKS. N.P., N.D. WEB.

PERFECT VISION:

BROWN, BRANDON P. MAGILL'S MEDICAL GUIDE. PASADENA, CA: SALEM, 2011. PRINT.

CHAPTER THREE: HOW THE COLORS ARE MADE UP IN THE SOUND OF THE VOICE

THE MAKE-UP OF COLORS:

HTTP://ACES.NMSU.EDU/PUBS/_C/C-316.HTML

THE EAR (PINNA):

MOSBY'S DICTIONARY OF MEDICINE, NURSING & HEALTH PROFESSIONS. ST. LOUIS, MO: MOSBY/ELSEVIER, 2009. PRINT.

COLOR THEORY:

HTTP://WWW.COLORMATTERS.COM/COLORTHEORY.HTML

CHAPTER FOUR: COLOR LAYERS OF SOUND AND THE SHAPE OF A VOICE

The Psychology of Colour:

http://www.eaglespiritministry.com/shared/tracy/pc.htm

Aura Archives:

http://www.alaskawellness.com/AuraArchive.htm

Color Meanings - Explore Palettes and Symbolism:

http://desktoppub.about.com/cs/color/a/symbolism.htm

The definition of pastel:

Chilvers, Ian. *The Oxford Dictionary of Art*. Oxford: Oxford UP, 2004. Print.

The definition of vibrant:

Free-form:

Merriam-Webster's Collegiate Dictionary. Springfield, MA: Merriam-Webster, 2008. Print.

CHAPTER FIVE: SENTENCES AND WORDS AND MUSIC NOTES

ACTIVATOR AND AMPLIFIER—JAMES C. MCKINNEY, FIVE PRACTICAL LESSONS IN SINGING, ISBN CONVENTION PRESS, NASHVILLE, TN, 1982.

EUSTACHIAN TUBE PROBLEMS:

BLUESTONE, CHARLES D., AND MARIA B. BLUESTONE. EUSTACHIAN TUBE: STRUCTURE, FUNCTION, ROLE IN OTITIS MEDIA. HAMILTON, ONT.: BC DECKER, 2005. PRINT.

VOWELS:

HTTP://WWW.ANCIENTSCRIPTS.COM/PHONETICS.HTML

SYNESTHESIA:

CAMPEN, CRÉTIEN VAN. THE HIDDEN SENSE: SYNESTHESIA IN ART AND SCIENCE. CAMBRIDGE, MA: MIT, 2008. PRINT.

CHAPTER SIX: BACKGROUND COLORS OF MOODS AND FEELINGS

CHAPTER SEVEN: OUTLINE OF A VOICE STUDY

INSTRUMENTS:

RANDEL, DON MICHAEL. THE HARVARD DICTIONARY OF MUSIC. CAMBRIDGE, MA: BELKNAP OF HARVARD UP, 2003. PRINT.

DRUMS:

NICHOLLS, GEOFF. THE DRUM BOOK: A HISTORY OF THE ROCK DRUM KIT. NEW YORK, NY: ICEBACKBEAT, 2008. PRINT.

VOICE FREQUENCIES:

WAGNER, MICHAEL J. INTRODUCTORY MUSICAL ACOUSTICS. RALEIGH, NC: CONTEMPORARY PUB., 1994. PRINT.

HODGES, DONALD A. HANDBOOK OF MUSIC PSYCHOLOGY. SAN ANTONIO: IMR, 1996. PRINT.

SCHNUPP, JAN, ISRAEL NELKEN, AND ANDREW KING. AUDITORY NEUROSCIENCE: MAKING SENSE OF SOUND. CAMBRIDGE, MA: MIT, 2012. PRINT.

CHAPTER EIGHT: SINGING VOICE

CARE OF THE VOICE:

CAZDEN, JOANNA. EVERYDAY VOICE CARE: THE LIFESTYLE GUIDE FOR SINGERS AND TALKERS. N.P.: N.P., N.D. PRINT.

GREENE, ALAN, PAMELA HYDE, AND SUSAN GREENE. THE NEW VOICE: HOW TO SING AND SPEAK PROPERLY. [UNITED STATES]: CHAPPELL/INTERSONG MUSIC GROUP-USA, 1975. PRINT.

NON-VERBAL COMMUNICATIONS:

KARPF, ANNE. THE HUMAN VOICE: HOW THIS EXTRAORDINARY INSTRUMENT REVEALS ESSENTIAL CLUES ABOUT WHO WE ARE. NEW YORK: BLOOMSBURY PUB., 2006. PRINT.

MEHRABIAN, ALBERT. NONVERBAL COMMUNICATION. NEW BRUNSWICK, NJ: ALDINE TRANSACTION, 2007. PRINT.

VOCAL RANGES:

VOICE TYPE:

HINES, JEROME. THE FOUR VOICES OF MAN. NEW YORK: LIMELIGHT EDITIONS, 1997. PRINT.

EHMANN, WILHELM, AND FRAUKE HAASEMANN. VOICE BUILDING FOR CHOIRS. CHAPEL HILL, NC: HINSHAW MUSIC, 1982. PRINT.

GOETZE, MARY, ANGELA BROEKER, AND RUTH BOSHKOFF. EDUCATING YOUNG SINGERS: A RESOURCE FOR TEACHER-CONDUCTORS. NEW PALESTINE, IN: MJ, 2009. PRINT.

ABSOLUTE PITCH:

TANEDA, NAOYUKI, AND RUTH TANEDA. EDUCATION FOR ABSOLUTE PITCH: A NEW WAY TO LEARN PIANO : HANDBOOK FOR TEACHERS AND PARENTS FOR THE WE HEAR AND PLAY SYSTEM. GAINESVILLE, FL: ACOUSTIC LEARNING, 2005. PRINT.

ARONSON, ARNOLD E., AND DIANE M. BLESS. CLINICAL VOICE DISORDERS. NEW YORK: THIEME, 2009. PRINT.

SAPIENZA, CHRISTINE M., AND RUDDY BARI. HOFFMAN. VOICE DISORDERS. SAN DIEGO: PLURAL PUB., 2013. PRINT.

BOONE, DANIEL R., STEPHEN C. MCFARLANE, AND RICHARD I. ZRAICK. THE VOICE AND VOICE THERAPY. N.P.: N.P., N.D. PRINT.

MECHANICAL LARYNX:

JAMA NETWORK | JAMA | A MECHANICAL LARYNX

A MECHANICAL LARYNX

E. I. MCKESSON, M.D.

JAMA. 1927;88(9):645-646.
DOI:10.1001/JAMA.1927.92680350028011B.

DYSLEXIA:

RIEF, SANDRA F., AND JUDITH M. STERN. THE DYSLEXIA CHECKLIST: A PRACTICAL REFERENCE FOR PARENTS AND TEACHERS. SAN FRANCISCO, CA: JOSSEY-BASS, 2010. PRINT.

ALZHEIMER'S DISEASE:

PARKINSON'S DISEASE:

AMYOTROPHIC LATERAL SCLEROSIS (ALS, OR LOU GEHRIG'S DISEASE):

MULTIPLE SCLEROSIS:

NETTINA, SANDRA M. LIPPINCOTT MANUAL OF NURSING PRACTICE. PHILADELPHIA: WOLTERS KLUWER HEALTH, 2010. PRINT.

HUNTINGTON'S DISEASE:

QUARRELL, OLIVER. HUNTINGTON'S DISEASE. OXFORD: OXFORD UP, 2008. PRINT.

CHAPTER THIRTEEN: THE EAR

EAR STRUCTURE:

CLARK, WILLIAM W., AND KEVIN K. OHLEMILLER. ANATOMY AND PHYSIOLOGY OF HEARING FOR AUDIOLOGISTS. CLIFTON PARK, NY: THOMSON DELMAR, 2008. PRINT.

ECHOLOCATION:

JOHNSON, TIM, AND JUSTIN LOUCHART. BEGINNER'S GUIDE TO ECHOLOCATION FOR THE BLIND AND VISUALLY IMPAIRED: LEARNING TO SEE WITH YOUR EARS. N.P.: N.P., N.D. PRINT.

SCHNUPP, JAN, ISRAEL NELKEN, AND ANDREW KING. AUDITORY NEUROSCIENCE: MAKING SENSE OF SOUND. CAMBRIDGE, MA: MIT, 2012. PRINT.

CHAPTER FOURTEEN: CAUSES OF HEARING LOSS

FREQUENCY RANGE OF HUMAN HEARING:

HTTP://HYPERTEXTBOOK.COM/FACTS/2003/CHRISDAMBROSE.SHT ML

HEARING AIDS:

DILLON, HARVEY. HEARING AIDS. SYDNEY: BOOMERANG, 2012. PRINT.

EVANS, ALFRED S., AND RICHARD A. . KASLOW. VIRAL INFECTIONS OF HUMANS. NEW YORK: PLENUM CORPORATION, 1997. PRINT.

PRESBYCUSIS:

AUDITORY FATIGUE:

TINNITUS:

OSTEITIS:

DUGAN, MARCIA B. LIVING WITH HEARING LOSS. WASHINGTON, D.C.: GALLAUDET UP, 2003. PRINT.

CHAPTER FIFTEEN: OTHER VOICES, WORDS, SAYINGS, AND CHANGING COLORS

BIRDS:

PARROTS:

BIRD COMMUNICATION:

SOUCEK, GAYLE. AMAZON PARROTS: A COMPLETE PET OWNER'S MANUAL. HAUPPAGE, NY: BARRON'S EDUCATIONAL SERIES, 2010. PRINT.

KROODSMA, DONALD E., EDWARD H. MILLER, AND HENRI OUELLET. ACOUSTIC COMMUNICATION IN BIRDS. NEW YORK: ACADEMIC, 1982. PRINT.

ORIGIN OF LANGUAGE:

HOFFMAN, JOEL M. IN THE BEGINNING: A SHORT HISTORY OF THE HEBREW LANGUAGE. NEW YORK: NEW YORK UP, 2006. PRINT.

LANGUAGES OF THE WORLD:

ABLEY, MARK. SPOKEN HERE: TRAVELS AMONG THREATENED LANGUAGES. BOSTON: MARINER ., 2005. PRINT.

PERSONALITY:

SCHIZOPHRENIA:

TOURETTE SYNDROME:

SELECTIVE MUTISM:

DIAGNOSTIC AND STATISTICAL MANUAL OF MENTAL DISORDERS. WASHINGTON, DC: AMERICAN PSYCHIATRIC ASSOCIATION, 1994. PRINT.

CAT COMMUNICATION:

HTTP://WWW.PETS.CA/ARTICLES/ARTICLE-CATCOMMUNIC.HTM

LEARNING HAWAIIAN:

WIGHT, KAHIKĀHEALANI. LEARN HAWAIIAN AT HOME. HONOLULU, HI: BESS, 2005. PRINT.

LEARNING RUSSIAN:

BEYER, THOMAS R. LEARN RUSSIAN THE FAST AND FUN WAY. HAUPPAUGE, NY: BARRON'S, 2009. PRINT.

LEARNING HEBREW:

YEDWAB, PAUL MICHAEL., AND HOWARD BOGOT. LEARN HEBREW TODAY: ALEF-BET FOR ADULTS. NEW YORK, NY: UAHC, 1992. PRINT.

ANIMAL INFO

BLUE WHALE:

CALAMBOKIDIS, JOHN, AND GRETCHEN STEIGER. BLUE WHALES. STILLWATER, MN: VOYAGEUR, 1997. PRINT.

CHAMELEON:

"CHAMELEONS: NATURE'S HIDDEN JEWELS [HARDCOVER]." CHAMELEONS: NATURE'S HIDDEN JEWELS: PETR NECAS: 9781575241371: AMAZON.COM: BOOKS. N.P., N.D. WEB. 08 JULY 2013.

SQUID:

CEPHALOPODS:

CUTTLEFISH:

WILLIAMS, WENDY. KRAKEN: THE CURIOUS, EXCITING, AND SLIGHTLY DISTURBING SCIENCE OF SQUID. NEW YORK: ABRAMS IMAGE, 2011. PRINT.

OCTOPUS:

MATHER, JENNIFER A., ROLAND C. ANDERSON, AND JAMES B. WOOD. OCTOPUS: THE OCEAN'S INTELLIGENT INVERTEBRATE. PORTLAND, OR.: TIMBER, 2010. PRINT.

CHAPTER SIXTEEN: FACTS OF COLORS IN WHAT YOU SEE AND HEAR EVERYDAY

GEORGE WASHINGTON:

ELLIS, JOSEPH J. HIS EXCELLENCY: GEORGE WASHINGTON. NEW YORK: VINTAGE, 2005. PRINT.

HTTP://THELONGESTLISTOFTHELONGESTSTUFFATTHELONGESTDOMAINNAMEATLONGLAST.COM/TRIVIA93.HTML

SLEEP TALKING:

HUNTER, SAMANTHA. TALKING IN YOUR SLEEP--. TORONTO: HARLEQUIN, 2007. PRINT.

CHAPTER SEVENTEEN: THE COLORS OF LIFE EXPERIENCES

MOOD RINGS:

HTTP://WWW.SHEOFMERMAIDS.BLOGSPOT.COM

MEANINGS OF THE DIFFERENT COLORS OF ROSES:

HTTP://WWW.ROSE-GARDENING-MADE-EASY.COM/DIFFERENT-COLOR-ROSES-SYMBOLIZE.HTML

CHAPTER EIGHTEEN: VOICES IN DREAMS

VIGO, MICHAEL. WHAT'S IN YOUR DREAM?: AN A TO Z DREAM DICTIONARY. [S.L.]: DREAM MOODS, 2010. PRINT.

PEIRCE, PENNEY. DREAMS FOR DUMMIES. FOSTER CITY, CA: IDG WORLDWIDE, 2001. PRINT.

CHAPTER NINETEEN: DIFFERENT KINDS OF THERAPIES

COLOR THERAPY:

GHADIALI, DINSHAH P. SPECTRO-CHROME METRY ENCYCLOPEDIA: HOME TRAINING COURSE IN SPECTRO-CHROME METRY : THE SCIENCE OF AUTOMATIC PRECISION. MALAGA, NJ: DINSHAH HEALTH SOCIETY, 2003. PRINT.

ANDERSON, MARY, AND MARY ANDERSON. COLOUR THERAPY. N.P.: AQUARIAN, 1990. PRINT.

COLOR AND MOOD:

HTTP://WWW.NYDAILYNEWS.COM/LIFESTYLE/2009/02/10/2009-02-10_WANT_A_MOOD_SWING_CHANGE_YOUR_COLORS.HTML

SOUND THERAPY:

DAVIS, DORINNE S. SOUND BODIES THROUGH SOUND THERAPY. LANDING, NJ: KALCO PUB., 2004. PRINT.

GOLDMAN, JONATHAN. HEALING SOUNDS: THE POWER OF HARMONICS. ROCHESTER, VT: HEALING ARTS, 2002. PRINT.

MUSIC THERAPY:

MUSIC AND MELODIC INTONATION THERAPY:

ISO PRINCIPLE:

DAVIS, WILLIAM B., KATE E. GFELLER, AND MICHAEL H. THAUT. AN INTRODUCTION TO MUSIC THERAPY: THEORY AND PRACTICE. DUBUQUE, IA: WM. C. BROWN, 1992. PRINT.

GUIDED IMAGERY AND MUSIC (GIM):

BRUSCIA, KENNETH E., AND DENISE ERDONMEZ. GROCKE. GUIDED IMAGERY AND MUSIC: THE BONNY METHOD AND BEYOND. GILSUM, NH: BARCELONA PUB., 2002. PRINT.

CHAPTER TWENTY: VOICE TECHNOLOGIES

Electronic voice phenomenon:

Taylor, Troy. *Ghost Hunter's Guidebook: The Essential Guide to Investigating Ghosts & Hauntings*. Decatur, IL: Whitechapel Productions, 2007. Print.

Voice recognition interface:

Cohen, Michael H., James P. Giangola, and Jennifer Balogh. *Voice User Interface Design*. Boston: Addison-Wesley, 2004. Print.

Global positioning system (GPS):

El-Rabbany, Ahmed. *Introduction to GPS: The Global Positioning System*. Boston, MA: Artech House, 2002. Print.

Vocoder and Talk box:

Kondoz, A. M. *Digital Speech: Coding for Low Bit Rate Communication Systems*. Chichester: Wiley, 2004. Print.

CONCLUSION